RETIREMENT PLANNING GUIDE

10 Steps to Generate Steady Income, Plan Strategic Investments, and Build An Emotional Fulfilling Life on Any Budget

JD WILLIAMS

Copyright © 2023 JD Williams

All rights reserved. No part of this publication may be reproduced, distributed, or transmitted in any form or by any means, including photocopying, recording, or other electronic or mechanical methods, without the prior written permission of the publisher, except in the case of brief quotations embodied in critical reviews and certain other non-commercial uses permitted by copyright law.

 **CONTENTS**

Introduction 5

1. Assess Your Current Financial State vs. Your Retirement Plan 9
2. Readjust Your Savings with Broader Investment Options for Anyone 25
3. Tackle Your Liabilities Sooner rather than Later 35
4. Plan and Save for Expenses and Emergencies in Retirement 45
5. Budget Properly through Every Step Before and After Retirement . 59
6. Retirement Plan Pitfalls to Avoid for Security and Wellness 70
7. Create A Steady Income to Complement Your Retirement Years ... 83
8. Look After Yourself Physically and Mentally to Enjoy Retirement 97
9. Give Yourself A Purpose and Dream Big without Spending Money 109
10. Transform Your Legacy into Inspiration for others and Loved Ones 123

Conclusion 137

References 141

Introduction

Many of us tend to think of retirement as a distant milestone, something that will happen in the distant future. However, the reality is that by 2030, all Baby Boomers will have reached retirement age. By 2045, every member of Generation X will have done the same. It's concerning that only 77% of Americans are investing in 401K plans, and a substantial 60% will heavily rely on Social Security benefits post-retirement. Given that Social Security may not be sufficient to support your retirement lifestyle, it's crucial to give serious thought to your retirement planning.

If you're concerned about your retirement future, you're not alone. Worries about running out of savings, handling unexpected emergencies, or managing existing debt are common. Nobody wants to feel like they'll become a burden to their family in retirement or have to compromise drastically on their lifestyle and dreams. You might even question whether you possess all the necessary knowledge to plan for retirement. It's a subject rarely covered in schools or workplaces, so feeling a bit lost is entirely natural.

Just thinking about retirement can be stressful, with fears, anxieties, and uncertainties looming large. The good news is that you can address these concerns with a well-structured, practical plan. This retirement planning guide offers step-by-step assistance to help you steer your planning efforts and experience greater peace of mind. This book will walk you through ten steps, from initially knowing very little about retirement planning to developing an effective strategy that enables you to relish your golden years and leave a legacy for your loved ones.

I personally wasn't prepared for retirement before I started following the steps in this book. Regrettably, I made more mistakes than I care to admit, squandering precious years that could have been dedicated to planning for a more secure future. I had to shake myself off and become proactive. I threw myself into learning about the essential requirements for retirement, how to plan effectively, and ensuring I had multiple strategies to lead me toward a desirable retirement. I recognized that not everything is within our control, but there are aspects that you can manage. With the guidance provided in this book, you'll feel empowered, no matter where you stand at the moment.

With practical tools, the right knowledge, and the step-by-step instructions in this book, you can move from feeling uncertain to confident and capable of managing the controllable aspects as your retirement approaches. These methods will help you chart every aspect of your retirement journey, including budgeting, debt management, and more. You'll also learn how to maintain a stable income post-retirement without taking undue risks in a volatile market. Of course, there's room for some calculated risks, but these should be ones you're comfortable managing to achieve stability and purpose.

My aim is to assist you in avoiding the mistakes and missteps I made on my own journey. I stumbled many times before discovering the steps that worked for me and others. Given the continuously shifting global economy, I needed a plan that allowed flexibility to adapt to economic changes. It took me a while to understand that a plan couldn't be set in stone, but I learned from my past errors and became more mindful of self-management. With this book, you can benefit from my experience and sidestep the pitfalls on your path to retirement and future planning. You can use these steps to create a practical plan for your retirement, no matter where you are in life right now. Whether you're in your thirties, forties, or approaching retirement age, the straightforward steps in this book can benefit you.

So, if you're ready to embrace change and take a proactive approach to your retirement planning, alleviating the pressures that might otherwise force you to work harder and longer, let's dive into the first of the ten steps, which will provide you with practical advice and tools.

CHAPTER 1

Assess Your Current Financial State vs. Your Retirement Plan

"You cannot escape the responsibility of tomorrow by evading it today."
- Abraham Lincoln

Trying to make crucial decisions when you don't have all the necessary information is almost asking for failure. Despite this, according to data from the U.S. Census Bureau, approximately 50% of people aged 55 to 66 don't see how their current finances will impact their retirement plans. This information means that millions of Americans are not financially prepared for retirement.

Being unprepared is typical of not fully appreciating your current financial situation. But fear of the future will only show you whether it looks good or bad. The key to planning for a better tomorrow is to assess everything today.

In this chapter, we'll help you assess your current financial situation, as you won't be able to make changes if you don't fully appreciate what could be wrong. This step will help you to evaluate your retirement plans so you can make sure that you remain on track.

Although the idea may seem daunting, an assessment will allow you to identify any changes you need to make. It can expose any potential problems or shortfalls in the coming years.

Calculate Your Savings and Funds:

Several stages are involved in performing these checks to get a clear picture of your overall savings and funds. These include:

Evaluate Your Current Assets:

Take a few moments to review the current savings. You must look at your entire assets, including 401K, IRAs, brokerage accounts, etc. Most people don't know, off the top of their heads, what funds they have or where the money is held. You will likely have multiple accounts, so you must list everything and add them together.

Revisit Your Retirement Plans:

This step is very personal, as your ideas of retirement bliss may differ significantly from someone else's. You'll need to ask yourself several questions to understand your future plans better. What are your plans for housing? Will you remain in your current property or downsize? Will a vacation home become your full-time home after you retire?

Since health issues are more common as we age, you will also need to consider what measures you can put in place should you suffer any health issues. The option could be a care plan or a separate fund to cover your medical costs.

Determining what funds you will need is difficult, but a rough estimate is beneficial for evaluating. You could use your existing spending as a guide, but remember that your day-to-day costs are likely to change. For Example, you won't have the cost of a daily commute, but you may want to socialize more often. Think about how you imagine spending your days during retirement and try to estimate the potential costs involved.

Gather All Your Pension Information:

You must gather all the paperwork and details about your pension plans. This step includes your plan information, retirement investments, and savings, including movable assets and property.

This information will help you identify the various income sources you'll have in retirement. If you're close to retirement, you can also look at government benefits and Social Security, which you will be eligible for.

Assess Your Current Savings Rate:

Next, you must look realistically at how much you save each year. While many experts quote percentages of how much you should save, look at what you are actually keeping.

Please keep all the details from the above steps, as we will need them for the calculations and comparisons later in this chapter.

I'll provide some Examples to help you put the above into context.

Example One:

Lisa is 50, her home is worth $218,000, her yearly income is $55,600, and she contributes 10% to her 401K.

Account	Balance
401K	$130,000
IRA	$38,000
CD	$10,000
Emergency Fund Savings Account	$5,000
Total for Retirement Savings	$178,000

Lisa estimates her retirement lifestyle will cost approximately $50,000 in today's terms per year. She hopes to maintain this lifestyle for about 30 years, and considering future inflation, her retirement funds fall short of the total amount she'll need.

Example Two:

Bob and Mary are a married couple with a home worth approximately $268,000. Bob is 53, and Mary is 50. They have two children in college who will graduate in two years. The annual income for Bob and Mary is $78,000 and $44,000 respectively. They currently pay $15,000 annually to help their children with their educational expenses and pay 6% of their incomes into their 401K.

	Bob	Mary
401K	$301,000	$106,000
IRA	$45,000	$34,000
Stocks	$25,000	
Bonds		$11,000
Emergency Fund Savings	$5,500	$2,100
Total for Retirement Savings	$371,000	$151,000

Bob and Mary plan to downsize to a less expensive home for retirement and anticipate retirement costs of approximately $50,000 per year.

With total retirement savings of $522,000 and the potential for adding more from the sale of their current home, Bob and Mary are close to being on track with their retirement planning.

Example Three:

Laurie is 62 and divorced; the couple did not tend to save while married. Her condo is worth approximately $105,000, and her annual income from Social Security is $30,600. However, she is starting a small online business to compensate for lost time and contribute to her retirement income. Her business could offer $2,000 to $5,000 per month.

401K	$154,000
Savings Account (Emergency)	$5,000
Total for Retirement Savings	$154,000

Laurie wants to maintain her current standard of living after retirement. Still, she wants to save some money for one or two budget vacations each year. Unless Laurie's business starts bringing in serious income, she needs to make profound changes to her retirement plans.

Example Four:

Helen is 45 and has a home which is worth approximately $165,000. Her annual income is $53,000, and she currently contributes $7,000 annually to her 401K.

401K	$106,000
IRA	$48,000
Stocks	$57,000
Emergency Fund Savings	$4,300
Total for Retirement Savings	$211,000

Helen has a total retirement savings of $211,000. She plans to retire overseas and have a lower cost of living of approximately $36,000 per year. Even if she sells her home to move abroad, Helen falls short of her retirement needs.

Write Down Your Liabilities:

It's the time to gather the details for all your liabilities. Many people find this topic daunting, but it is necessary for a clear picture of your current financial situation and how it will impact your retirement plans.

Calculate Pre-Retirement Debts:

It's a good starting point because while you may feel confident that you can quickly pay off these debts, they will impact your savings ability right now. Your debts may include credit cards, store cards, personal loans, auto loans, or other short to medium-term credit accounts.

Evaluate Your Mortgage Account:

Next, you must pull out your latest mortgage statement to check your balance. Many people know how long their mortgage deal was for initially, but they need to track how many years remain on the account. This scenario applies if you've remortgaged over the years or taken on additional debt secured on your home.

Your mortgage statement will break down the current balance and detail the remaining months. You can also see the amount of interest charged to the account each month. It will also show how the remaining months will bring down the balance of your account to zero, so you can see how long remains on your mortgage and what it would cost you to pay it off early, if necessary.

Gather Your Education Debt:

Whether you have outstanding college loans or student debt or need to cover your children's education costs, this debt will impact your retirement savings and future retirement plans. According to Federal Reserve data, since 2017, educational debt within the 50 to 61 age group in the U.S. has increased by 33.5%, with an average debt of $45,754. Generally, you cannot discharge federal student loans even if you declare bankruptcy. In a worst-case scenario, your Social Security could be forfeited if you don't pay on time. Additionally, the interest on educational debt may not be tax deductible.

Gather Information on Other Liabilities:

You will also need to gather information on any other liabilities that you may currently have. Your list of other liabilities could include credit cards, personal loans, or auto loans. Suppose you have any accounts with a negative balance we have not covered above. In that case, you must note the outstanding amounts for each account. It will help you to have a clear picture of your total liabilities.

Calculate Your Monthly Obligations:

Now that you've gathered all the information on your various liabilities, you can check your statements to calculate your monthly obligations. In many cases, this will be a fixed amount, such as a mortgage or personal loan payment. But with credit cards or other types of debt, you can have a variable payment or a minimum amount you must pay each month.

It is a good idea to categorize all of your expenses from your statements into fixed or flexible payments. It will help you in the assessment phase of your retirement planning journey and when you develop an action plan in the later steps.

It is best to err on the side of caution and round up any amounts you must pay each month. Keep the list of these expenses close to hand, as you will need the details of these liabilities later.

Examples:

For the below Examples, the assumption is that we use only the total yearly income as net income after tax to make it easier to understand.

Lisa:

Liability	Monthly Payment
Mortgage	$865 with 10 years remaining
Utilities	$405 to $500
Car Insurance	$75
Car Payments	$455 with three years remaining
Home Improvement Loan ($20k Loan)	$381 with three years remaining
Life Insurance	$385 for the next 12 years
Home Insurance	$1,231 per year
HOA	$635 per year
Property Tax	$3,351 per year
Credit Card One (balance $3,871 at 21% APR)	$158 per month
Credit Card Two (balance $2,361 at 21% APR)	$158 per month

Lisa's expenses are $40,941 per year for at least the next three years. With her annual income of $55,600 and her 10% contribution to her 401K, Lisa only has approximately $9,099 of her income remaining each year.

Bob and Mary:

Liability	Monthly Payment
Mortgage	$894 for the next five years
Utilities	$605 to $700
Property Tax	$4,457 per year
HOA	$585 per year
Car Payments	$561 for the next five years
Car Insurance	$165
Personal Loan- Bob (balance of $10,871)	$275 for the next four years
Bob Credit Card One ($2,573 balance at 24% APR)	$45
Mary Credit Card One ($2,361 balance at 21% APR)	$75
Mary Credit Card Two ($654 balance at 21% APR)	$25

Bob and Mary's combined expenses add up to $37,922 for at least the next four years. With their combined salaries of $122,000, 401K contributions, and children's education costs, Bob and Mary have almost 50% of their salary left after covering their financial obligations.

Laurie:

Liability	Monthly Payment
Condo HOA (which includes her home structure insurance & all utilities)	$865
Utilities	$95
Property Tax	$3,018 per year
Property Contents Insurance	$360 per year
Credit Card One: Balance of $9,876 at 21% APR for business expenses	$271
Credit Card Two: Balance of $3,341 at 21% APR for personal expenses	$91

Laurie has total liabilities of $19,242 per year, approximately 65% of her income. But her new business should increase her available income in the near future.

Helen:

Liability	Monthly Payment
Mortgage	$698 for the next 15 years
Utilities	$605 to $700
HOA	$585 per year
Property Tax	$3,875 per year
Home Insurance	$1,135 per year

Car Insurance	$75
Credit Card One: Balance $4,361 at 21% APR	$180
Credit Card Two: Balance $1,371 at 21% APR	$55

Helen's liabilities add up to $26,091 annually, just less than 50% of her annual income. It provides her with additional funds to increase her retirement planning.

Assess Your Retirement Longevity Risk:

The next stage involves assessing your longevity risk for retirement. While we all may imagine living past the century mark, planning your retirement on this basis may place you under greater strain and add to your stress. When planning for retirement, you need a more accurate longevity estimate to make informed decisions about drawing down savings, claiming pension benefits, and avoiding outliving your assets.

The term "longevity risk" is used within the insurance industry to estimate life expectancy and survival rates. Life insurance costs you more as you age; you are statistically more likely to die than someone younger. However, longevity risk must be a major consideration in your retirement planning.

Longevity risk affects your pension funds, not only in how long your savings may last but how much you should draw down each month. For Example, while two people may have the same $500,000 pension fund, if one is estimated to live until 75 and the other has a projected lifespan of 85, the latter will need to make his fund last 10 additional years.

While there are no guarantees in life, it is possible to make provisions so you don't outlive your retirement income. You must consider whether you want to buy annuities or practice self-management. For Example, the 4% rule is a withdrawal strategy to minimize longevity risk. Essentially, it means that you draw down a maximum of 4% of the total value of your retirement savings in the first year and adjust for inflation in the following years. For Example, if you have $1 million in your 401K, you could withdraw a maximum of $40,000 in the first year. If the inflation rate in year two is 2%, you could adjust your withdrawal amount and increase the maximum to $40,800. You may also need to check your insurance policies to see if you need to make changes if the longevity risk is inappropriate.

In our above Examples, Lisa has family members who live up to 85, so she has taken out a life insurance policy offering $1 million with long-term care. On the other hand, Bob and Mary don't have life insurance. Bob's family tend to die in their late 60s, while Mary's family members have lived to 80. It means Mary may be vulnerable, as Bob will likely have a shorter longevity risk.

Neither Laurie nor Helen has life insurance; Laurie's family members tend to live to age 80, while Helen's live to 70. Both of them are vulnerable if they suffer from health issues after retirement.

Keep all of these details on hand to help you to gain awareness during this assessment.

Final Assessment:

In this assessment stage, we determine what you want to achieve with your financial retirement plans and what you want to save. It is the ideal time to start making your retirement goals.

Everyone has a different way of imagining their retirement. You may envisage yourself taking luxury vacations several times a year. In contrast, others may want to be homebodies who enjoy socializing within their community and helping out with grandchildren. Both these scenarios will require a different level of income.

Use your current expenses to guide how much income you must have to maintain a similar lifestyle, making the appropriate adjustments according to your goals. You will then need to project how much savings you will need to achieve this lifestyle after you retire. A good rule of thumb is considering maximum withdrawals of 4% to 5% of your portfolio value each year. So, if you'll need $50,000 a year, you'll need $1.25 million in assets.

Fortunately, some simple investment calculators can help you determine the precise amounts customized to your retirement goals. For Example, Bank Rate [1] has a superb calculator that is free. You need to enter your current savings and a few other details to calculate how much you'll need to reach your necessary retirement fund.

Bear in mind that if you reduce your liabilities and debt before retirement, you can decrease the amount you will realistically need to survive each month. In the Examples covered above, by the time Lisa reaches the age of 65, she will no longer be making a mortgage payment, her car finance and home improvement loan.

Setting goals for how much you want to save for housing, healthcare, long-term care insurance, an emergency fund, and other long-term provisions is also a good idea.

You can use all of these figures in a retirement calculator to see what changes you need to make to align with your goals. There is a great calculator on Dave Ramsey's official website, RamseySolutions.com [2]. You must enter your current age, projected retirement age, and some of your figures to check if your retirement fund is on track.

If we enter the details from our Examples into this calculator, you can see that Lisa would have a projected retirement fund of $2,865,149. Suppose Bob and Mary have a joint retirement fund. In that case, their projected portfolio will total $3,748,030 plus whatever funds they add from downsizing their home.

This type of calculator can be remarkably helpful in assessing whether your retirement savings are on track and what else you need to do to ensure you have sufficient income to support your retirement goals.

Fernando Flores, Finance Minister for Chile, entrepreneur, and engineer, once said, "I made my assessment of my life, and I began to live it. That was freedom." By assessing your current situation, you can start to get control of your finances and open up the path to the coming steps in this book, ensuring that you make the changes that will benefit your freedom in your golden years. Any professional financial planner will begin with assessing your current finances, so this is always a good place to start. Once you know any potential issues, we can move on to the next step to begin correcting them.

YOUR RETIREMENT WORKSHEET:

List all your retirement accounts (401K, IRA, Stocks, Bonds, etc…)

Type and Account#	You	Partner
Total for Retirement Savings		

YOUR LIABILITIES WORKSHEET:

List all your expenses (mortgage payment or rent, home insurance, property tax, HOA fee, lawn care, property improvement loan, car payments, car insurance, health insurance, life insurance, improvement loan, and any debts you still need to pay)

Type & How Often (Weekly, Bi-Weekly, Monthly, or Yearly)	Account Number	Amount	Calculated Yearly Amount
Total Liabilities			

CHAPTER 2

Readjust Your Savings With Broader Investment Options for Anyone

"The most important quality for an investor is temperament, not intellect."
— Warren Buffet

Before we can close the subject of retirement goals, we need to discuss various ways to maximize your current savings or add to plans to create more income for your retirement. According to a survey conducted by American Express, just over one-third of people have three or more retirement accounts, while only one in six have five or more accounts.

Although it may be tempting to try to simplify your retirement accounts, this could mean you're missing out on income-earning potential. So, in this chapter, we'll go through the many investment options that anyone can use to help you discover the best fit for your circumstances, preferences, and requirements.

For readers in countries other than the US, please use a similar investment plan in your home country.

Different Types of IRA

Most people know that IRAs are retirement accounts, but are you aware there are numerous IRA types? This makes it easier to find the IRA that best suits your circumstances. The IRA types include:

- **Traditional IRA**

    Traditional IRAs allow you to put aside pre-tax dollars. Any money you save will be taken from your income before the taxes are deducted. This lowers your taxable income, but you will be subject to paying taxes when you make withdrawals after you retire since you are just deferring the tax payments. There are limits to how much you can contribute, but over 50s can make additional payments.

- **Roth IRA**

    The Roth IRA is a great option for younger people as it can be funded with post-tax dollars. Although this removes the immediate tax deduction, you can avoid the significant income tax burden when you make withdrawals after retirement. Roth IRAs have the potential to be lucrative in the long run. But if retirement is fast approaching, you may not be able to take full advantage. Fortunately, those over 50 have a higher contribution limit, so you can have money sitting in your account earning more tax-free interest.

- **Rollover IRA**

    When you move a retirement account to a new IRA, you'll create a rollover IRA. Essentially, you're "rolling" the money from one account into your rollover IRA. However, a Rollover IRA can be a traditional or Roth IRA. Just be aware that transferring an IRA can create tax liabilities, so it is essential to check with a financial planner or tax advisor before you initiate the process.

- **SEP IRA**

    SEP IRAs are a little like a traditional IRA, but they are designed for small business owners and their teams. Self-employed people can also open a SEP IRA. Unlike some IRAs, only the employer can contribute to a SEP IRA, and the contributions go into a separate plan for each employee. The contributions can be made at the employer's discretion but capped at 25% of income or $66,000.

- **Simple IRA**

    The Simple IRA is an alternative for employees of small businesses that cannot provide access to a 401K. 401K's tend to be expensive to maintain. Hence, they are not practical for many businesses, but Simple IRAs work in a similar way. Employees can automatically save money through payroll deductions, and there is an option for employers to match these contributions. The amount is capped at 3% of the employee's annual salary, with an annual contribution limit set for each year. In 2023, this was $15,500, but if you're 50 or older, you can make catch-up contributions, which increase the limit to $19,000.

- **Spousal IRA**

    Although IRAs are typically reserved for workers earning income, as the name suggests, spousal IRAs allow the husband or wife of the worker to fund an IRA. The only caveat is that the spouse's taxable income needs to be higher than the contributions made to any IRA.

Create Your Own Plans

Fortunately, your retirement accounts are not limited to IRAs, as there are a number of other plans that may allow you to diversify and generate additional income streams. The choice of other plans includes:

- **Solo 401K**

    This is also called a solo-k, one participant-k, or Uni-k. Essentially, this plan is designed for business owners and their spouses. Since the business owner is both employer and employee, you can make elective deferrals and non-elective contributions. But, if you have plans to expand your business and take on employees, you can't use this plan.

- **GIAs:**

    Employers do not typically offer GIAs or guaranteed income annuities, but you can buy them to create your pension scheme. You can then trade a lump sum at retirement to purchase an immediate annuity and generate a monthly payment for life. You can buy GIAs after tax, so you will only need to pay tax on the earnings, or you can buy via an IRA for an upfront tax deduction.

- **Deferred Annuities**

    Deferred annuities are contracts offered by insurance companies. Essentially, they promise to pay a lump sum or regular income at a future date. You can use deferred annuities to supplement your retirement income.

    Three types of deferred annuities exist: variable, fixed, and indexed. Variable deferred annuities offer a return based on the portfolio of products the annuity owner chooses. In contrast, fixed ones promise a guaranteed rate of return. Indexed annuities provide a return based on a market index performance.

    All three operate on a tax-deferred basis, so you'll only pay tax when you withdraw or start receiving income.

Employer Offered Retirement Investments

If you are already employed, it may be worth investigating if you can access some retirement investments if they are offered by your company. These retirement investment products include:

- **Employer-Sponsored Plans (401K, 403b, and 457)**

    401K is the most popular type of retirement plan offered by major corporations. Still, 403B is used for employees of certain charities and public schools, and 457 plans are only available if you're an employee of a state or local government. These plans work similarly to qualified retirement plans, where the employer can match your investment up to a cap. For Example, if you deposit 2% of your annual income, your employer may deposit an equivalent amount. This means that if you can maximize your contributions, you'll get a bonus that will grow year on year. If you're over 50, you can also make catch-up contributions at an extra $7,500 per year.

    The funds in your account are not subject to income tax until you make a withdrawal. So, if you are approaching a higher tax bracket, you can get an immediate tax break.

- **Federal Thrift Savings Plans:**

    This type of plan is a little like a supercharged 401K, and it is available if you're a government worker or member of the uniformed services. You can choose from five investment options: a bond fund, a small cap fund, an international stock fund, an S&P 500 index fund, and a specially issued Treasury securities fund. All are low-cost so that you can make relatively easy investment decisions.

- **Traditional Pensions:**

    Traditional pensions are defined benefit plans, which are easy to manage as they are fully funded by your employer. These plans provide a fixed income when you retire, but you'll be lucky if your employer offers this type of product. Just 13 of Fortune 500 companies offer traditional pension plans to new employees.

    This is because these pensions are payable for life and are usually calculated according to your salary and length of service at the company. Essentially, they are an expensive promise that the employer needs to honor.

    So, if your employer offers a traditional pension, keep the plan active for as long as possible.

- **Cash Balance Plans:**

    These are another type of defined benefit plan. But rather than being offered an amount based on your income before retirement, your income is based on investment and contribution credits. For Example, if there is an investment credit or promise of a 5% return, the employer can decrease its contributions if the plan assets earn more. This creates flexibility and greater control over the costs of company pension schemes.

- **Cash Value Life Insurance Plans:**

    Some companies offer this type of plan as an employment benefit. These are available as whole life, universal life, variable universal life, or variable life. Essentially, they provide death benefits while building cash value, which can be used to support your retirement. If you make a withdrawal from the premiums you've paid, they are not subject to tax.

    These plans can be a little more complicated than others, but they can offer tax-free withdrawals if properly designed.

- **Simplified Employee Pensions**

    Often referred to as SARSEPs, these plans permit employee salary reduction contributions, but earnings can be withdrawn anytime. This is similar to the traditional IRA, but earnings and contributions can be rolled over tax-free into other retirement plans or IRAs.

    There are a number of restrictions imposed by the IRS for SARSEPs, so you would need to check with your employer if you qualify.

- **Employee Stock Ownership Plans**

    ESOPs are an employee benefit that gives you an ownership interest in your company as shares or stock. The plan is set up as a trust fund, but you can redeem your shares when you retire or terminate your employment.

Social Security Benefits

Social Security is often a primary income source for retirees, but there are ways to maximize your benefits to create a greater income. Firstly, you should aim to work for the full 35 years or more. Your benefits will be calculated according to your lifetime earnings, with an average indexed monthly earnings formula used to determine the specific amount. If you've had years where you've been unemployed, they will be calculated as zero, which will reduce your average.

Fortunately, you can replace those years by working after the age of 60. You can also delay your benefits to increase your earnings when you retire.

So, if you think that Social Security will form a crucial piece of your retirement income, it is well worth exploring how to maximize your benefits before you retire.

Employer-Sponsored Plans vs. Personal Investment

With so many retirement plans and products, figuring out which ones are best for you can be overwhelming. Pros and cons are associated with employer-sponsored plans and personal investment, so it is crucial to assess these to make an informed decision.

Employer-sponsored plans such as the 401K do offer some distinct benefits over personal investment plans. For Example, you can take your 401K to another employer if you change jobs or roll it into an IRA. This means you are not stuck with your employer simply because you don't want to lose your retirement benefits.

If you are happy sticking with the same company, defined benefit plans can offer income that won't run out. These types of plans offer payment until your death, so you won't outlive your income. You can also be invested in your company, so you can have a stake in the company's success.

In either type of plan, typically, you don't need to be involved in managing the fund. With most plans, your employer will take care of the fund management.

Personal investment plans typically offer higher contribution limits and the potential for investing in higher-return assets. You can usually invest in a more diverse choice of assets, but you'll need to take a more active role in managing the investment.

Choosing the Best Combination of Investment Options

Many opt for a 401K and an IRA, which offer two tax-advantaged retirement savings options. It is a good idea to have both options and try to max out your benefits, particularly if your employer matches your retirement contributions.

If you're saving into a 401K, aim to max out your employer match to enjoy an immediate return on your savings. Many employers will match 50 to

100 percent of your contributions per year, up to a maximum of approximately 3 to 5 percent of your salary.

Once you've maxed out your 401K, you should max out your IRA. If you have sufficient funds after these contributions, you can then look at other investment options. Topping out your accounts with the maximum legal amounts per year is the best strategy for your financial future. This will not only allow you to enjoy the tax advantages, but you can also compound your returns for greater income potential.

Having all your retirement funds in one account may seem simple, but it could reduce your future income potential. If you can invest in multiple accounts, you can spread the risk and increase your potential returns. Once you've identified the most appropriate products for your circumstances, it is time to incorporate debt management, making your retirement planning journey smoother.

CHAPTER 3

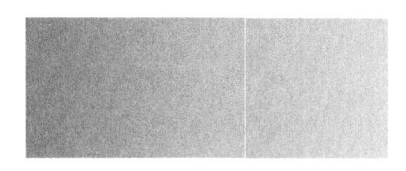

Tackle Your Liabilities Sooner Rather Than Later

"Debts are like children - begot with pleasure,
but brought forth with pain."
- MOLIERE

One of the main concerns for retirement planning is where to find the funds to invest for retirement or how to manage debt after retirement. If this applies to you, you're not alone. In fact, research shows that 71% of retirees have debt that is unrelated to their mortgage. Unfortunately, carrying debt in retirement can be a massive pitfall, as we'll cover in step six. But first, we will explore how you can reduce the risk of carrying debt into retirement.

Debt relief before retirement offers numerous benefits, including having more funds and savings to enjoy the lifestyle you're used to while retaining emergency funds. Retiring with debt can also impact not only your financial well-being but also your mental wellness [1]. Additionally, suppose you plan to retire without any outstanding liabilities. In that case, there is a higher risk of derailing your retirement plans, and you'll be more likely to use your retirement savings to service the debt.

JD Williams | 35

So, to reduce these risks and leverage the full benefits, you need to understand the basics of different debt management approaches and how they work.

Debt Management

Debt management can be a simple way to solve financial issues before retiring. The primary aim of debt management is to help you make a plan to pay off your debts, but it can also guide you on which debts you should focus on first. Your debt is organized according to the debt interest rate, terms, and other criteria. This type of planning can be very helpful to minimize the amount of interest you're paying on your outstanding debts.

For Example, if you have a credit card with a 29% interest rate and a personal loan with a 7% rate, a debt management program will likely prioritize paying off the credit card first. While your loan balance may be higher, you're probably accumulating far more interest charges on your credit card.

Therefore, the debt management program will be structured to continue paying the minimum necessary to the personal loan account. Still, any additional funds will be directed to your credit card account. Once the credit card account is cleared, there will be more funds to pay off your loan early.

Of course, many people have more complex finances than simply one credit card and one personal loan. This debt management program is a straightforward way to know what you should pay into each account monthly.

Debt management programs are typically created to clear your debts in 36 to 60 months. But sometimes, the debt management company can negotiate a rate freeze or other terms to help you clear the accounts efficiently.

Debt Counseling

Another option may be debt or credit counseling. This topic appears similar to debt management, but when you meet with a trained financial counselor, they make personalized recommendations after thoroughly reviewing your finances. The overall aim of this is to help you develop a better understanding of your financial situation and empower you to create an action plan. You are under no obligation to act on the recommendations. But you'll have a thorough review of all aspects of your finances, including your debt, savings, and assets.

There are several options for debt counseling, and you can speak to a counselor in person or over the phone. Since the counselor provides tailored recommendations, this service can give you a clear idea of how to clear your debt. Still, you'll have the flexibility to adjust your payments if something unexpected occurs.

For Example, while a debt management plan requires that you make specific monthly payments on all your accounts, debt counseling only offers recommendations of what you pay. If you have an unexpected car repair bill or need to replace a water heater, you can drop your payments down to the minimum due for a month or two to cover the cost.

Debt Consolidation

If you find managing multiple credit accounts a little overwhelming, you may want to consider debt consolidation. This approach means rolling all your debt into one loan to create only one monthly payment. The aim of debt consolidation is to make your financial journey smoother.

However, with any financial decision, there are pros and cons. You'll need to consider a few things before you make a final decision. Firstly, you'll need to look at the rate offered with a debt consolidation loan. If your credit score has recently dropped, you may be offered a loan with a higher interest rate than some of your credit accounts. You may obtain a lower rate by securing your new loan on your home or other assets. This option can be advantageous, but your home will be at risk if you can't stick to the repayment schedule.

You will also need to look at your debt consolidation loan terms. People considering debt consolidation often want to lower their monthly repayments. The goal is achieved by having the loan repayment cost less than the combined minimum payments across all the credit card accounts and loans. Unfortunately, this often means a longer-term loan, which, while offering some relief for your monthly expenses, may impact your timeline for retirement.

Debt management, counseling, or even debt consolidation can be viable if you consider dipping into your retirement savings. Carrying debt can feel overwhelming and stressful, but professional assistance can help you take control of your finances and be better prepared to organize your funds.

Debt Reduction

Consider a debt reduction program if none of the above options are feasible. Debt reduction offers short- and long-term plans to clear your debt according to your timeframe.

As the name suggests, the overall aim of debt reduction is to reduce your debt. There are professional service providers who specialize in debt reduction. As with the other methods we've covered above, you'll need to provide the details of your various accounts, and then the advisor will go through each to see where the debt can be effectively reduced.

In some circumstances, the advisor could negotiate a debt relief plan. The advisor will approach your credit card company, loan provider, or other creditor and see if they are willing to take a reduced amount to settle the account or if they would freeze the interest to enable you to pay down the account.

The advantage of this is that you can concentrate on paying off the account balance without worrying about more interest being added. However, there are some potential drawbacks, including the fact that your credit score may be impacted.

Some lenders will report the account as "paid-settled," letting future lenders know you negotiated a reduced balance to clear your account. So, suppose your retirement plans involve borrowing money. In that case, an official debt reduction plan may reduce the chances that you'll be approved for additional lending.

Self-Management of Your Debts

Ultimately, if you'd like to manage your debts, there are some self-management tools and strategies that you can use. Let's walk through the steps using the list of debts and liabilities you wrote down in step one.

Prioritize Your Debts

Although we've covered fixed and flexible debts in step one, prioritizing your debts is a little different. It would be best to sort your debts according to their liability and expense.

While it is easy to assume that you should pay off the largest debts first, this is not necessarily true. Often, the more significant debts, such as mortgages and loans, have fixed payments with a fixed term. This step lets you know exactly how much you need to pay and how long it takes to clear the account. On the other hand, credit cards have revolving debt. If you make the minimum payment due each month, you'll only pay a small amount off your overall balance. This case means that you could be carrying the debt for years!

In our earlier Examples, Lisa had a mortgage, a home improvement loan, car payments, and credit cards. Although her mortgage costs the most each month at $865, it will likely have the lowest interest rate, and the payments are fixed for the next ten years. However, both of Lisa's credit cards are at 21% APR, costing $316 per month. So, these should be Lisa's first priorities. After she clears these accounts, she could look at paying down her car and home improvement loans, which are fixed, with three years remaining. This scenario means that Lisa will have an end date when she no longer needs to cover these payments.

So, review your list of debts to see which should be your first priority with your debt repayment plan.

Calculate Your Debt Reduction Snowball

If you're unsure which liabilities should be prioritized, use a debt reduction snowball calculator. This tool can help you prioritize your debts, and it will help you budget in step five of this book.

Calculators like this one [2] are simple to use. You need to download your preferred format (either as a Google Sheet or Excel spreadsheet); you can then enter the details for your debts, and the spreadsheet will help you understand how a payment schedule will most effectively pay off your accounts. This tool can explore different strategies and determine which will work best for you.

Of course, it is possible to do this manually if you don't have access to a computer. Still, you'll need to do some serious calculations. You'll need to use the list of liabilities you created in step one and the APRs of each account, the monthly payments, and the terms. You can then use the loan payment formulae [3] to calculate the weight of your obligations.

Tackle Student Loans

As discussed earlier, educational debt is increasingly an issue for those nearing retirement. So, tackling your student loans or any educational loans you have for your children as soon as possible is important.

Unfortunately, you may have difficulty accessing the loan details if you're a co-signer on a loan for your children or grandchildren. After all, you'll only be responsible for the loan if your child or grandchild defaults on the payments. Fortunately, if the loans are federal student loans, you can visit the NSLDS (National Student Loan Data System) on the studentaid.gov website. Private loans can be trickier to find, but you can trace them by checking your credit report, which will show all your debts, including any educational loans you carry.

Once you know the balance and terms of the student loans, you'll need to consider how to retire without this debt. There are a few strategies to accomplish this. There are a few options for federal student loans, including the option to alter your repayment plan. It may also be possible to defer your loan or use forbearance, giving you some breathing room to prioritize other liabilities. Additionally, if you are disabled and the condition has not improved, you might have your loan discharged entirely.

If you're a co-signer on a loan, it is worth checking with the lender, as some allow the release of the co-signer once the primary borrower has made a set number of payments on time. So, if you co-signed for your child a few years ago, the chances are that you won't need to be responsible for the loan now.

If your debt is a private student loan, there are no standard relief options. However, lenders may allow negotiation of the repayment schedule.

Reduce Car Loans

Many people don't worry about car loans as they approach retirement. Typically, auto loans have a relatively low interest, fixed rate, meaning you'll know exactly how much you need to pay and for how long. However, there is the danger of these loans creeping up and compromising your retirement plans.

If you and your partner have a car loan, you'll be tying up a significant amount of money each month, which could be going toward your retirement goals or eating up a portion of your retirement income.

Firstly, you must consider whether you will need multiple vehicles in your household after retirement. You can manage with one car if you no longer need to drive to work every day. This option means you can sell the other car and get rid of one of your car loans. You will also no longer need to cover the cost of car insurance and upkeep on the second vehicle, so you could use these savings and the proceeds from the sale to pay down your remaining car loan.

If you need multiple vehicles in your household, consider trading in for less expensive models, which would reduce or eliminate your car loans. Remember that older vehicles can have higher maintenance and fuel costs, so this will need to be factored into your calculations.

Assess Your Mortgage and Home Loans

Clearing your mortgage before retirement may be an emotional decision rather than a strategic one. Still, many people enjoy the reassurance that they will not need to worry about repayments on their retirement income. Mortgage rates are typically low, so often, you can get better value investing rather than paying down your mortgage. However, if you're not on a fixed-rate deal, your finances can spiral out of control when rates increase.

This scenario happened to many homeowners throughout 2022 and 2023, when interest rates climbed significantly. So, it is understandable to worry that that small mortgage payment you could easily manage after retirement could become a financial burden.

Take a little time to assess your mortgage and any home loans to ensure you can comfortably clear them before your planned retirement date. If you fall short and your mortgage will continue past your retirement, consider making extra payments on the account to reduce the account balance.

Another strategy that is popular among retirees is to downsize. You could sell your current home and then use the proceeds to buy a less expensive or smaller home in full. This saving could reduce your financial burden, but a smaller home is easier to manage as you age.

Don't Put Retirement Savings on Hold

While tackling your debt and financial liabilities is essential, you mustn't put your retirement savings on hold. It is a common mistake to wait to save for retirement until all debt is paid off. It is unrealistic to think halting saving to make your debt disappear quicker will work for you in the long run. Since you need time for any investments from your retirement fund to bear fruit, waiting until the last moment to create a retirement account can be a big mistake.

It is more important to create a realistic budget, which allows you to pay down your debts strategically and put money away into your retirement fund. This option is where prioritizing your debts is crucial. You can concentrate on paying down debt that will be detrimental to your retirement rather than trying to clear all of your debt at the cost of your retirement savings.

Don't worry too much about planning and creating a budget for your debt repayment without putting your retirement savings on hold, as we will cover this in step five of this book.

Debt can be a burden at any time, but it can be incredibly stressful when trying to get your retirement planning on track. According to writer and engineer Michael Mihalik, it can also make a happy person bitter, and no one dreams of a bitter ending to their retirement. Fortunately, tackling your liabilities sooner rather than later can create a retirement filled with freedom and happy memories. By working on your debt and taking proactive action, you will be moving a step closer to achieving financial stability for your retirement. In the meantime, we will work on your savings for the planned and unexpected expenses in your retirement.

CHAPTER 4

Plan and Save for Expenses and Emergencies in Retirement

"You don't have to see the whole staircase, just take the first step.
— Martin Luther King, Jr.

The goals we've set in the previous steps are just the start, and it is now time to properly plan what you will need in retirement, including your savings and long-term care plans. A recent survey by the Society of Actuaries reported that approximately half of retirees experience some form of unexpected financial shock.

These unexpected expenses can seriously derail your retirement plans, so preparing yourself and your finances for any emergency is important. In this next step, you'll learn how to plan and save for expenses and emergencies to have the nest egg you may need.

Write Down All Your Post-Retirement Expenses

Before exploring how much money you will need in retirement, including some contingency for surprises, we need to delve into your necessary expenses. Your monthly living costs will be your number one priority, so you can continue living even if you face some financial issues.

Having covered your basic expenses in step one, we now need to review your anticipated post-retirement expenses that you'll need to cover monthly. These expenses will vary according to your circumstances, but the typical expenses you'll need to think about include:

- **Housing Costs**

    You must include this figure if you still have a mortgage or rent. However, even if you've paid off your mortgage, you still need to consider maintenance, property tax, and homeowner association fees. You can calculate these costs based on your current expenses.

- **Utilities**

    Gas, electricity, water, internet, phone, and other utilities can add up to one of the largest expenses retirees can face. Remember that you won't be out at work during the day once you're retired. Hence, your utilities may be slightly higher than your current bills, as you'll need to heat and cool your home for more hours per week.

- **Groceries and Food**

    This category can be easier to estimate since you can use your current expenses as a base. Remember that you have more time to prepare home meals rather than rely on more costly convenience foods.

- **Clothing**

    Even if you plan a leisurely retirement, you'll still need to update your closet periodically. So, it is essential to include clothing in your post-retirement budget.

- **Entertainment**

    This area should include dining out, movies, and other expenses in a typical month. You'll want to enjoy your retirement and not spend 24/7 inside your home. Whether you like to dine out with friends, see the latest movies, or have an evening at the theater, you must estimate how much you'll need per month.

- **Transportation**

    Although you won't be commuting to work every day, you will still need to factor in the cost of maintaining your vehicle, fuel, insurance, and repairs.

- **Travel**

    You can also budget travel into your post-retirement plans. Whether flying or driving, you'll need to cover all your travel costs, including hotels, spending money, and other expenses associated with your typical travel plans.

- **Health Care**

    This topic will likely be one of the most important categories in your post-retirement budget. Retirees spend an average of 5% of their monthly income on healthcare, with out-of-pocket expenses typically between $2,000 and $7,000 per year. Fidelity calculates that the average couple will need to budget $295,000 as an estimate for medical expenses, excluding long-term care in retirement.

    If you plan on using Medicare, you should be aware that while it will cover some of your healthcare costs in retirement, there are some limitations. You will still need to budget for premiums, deductibles, and other out-of-pocket expenses, including medications.

For Example, in 2023, the deductible for inpatient hospital treatment for Medicare Part A will be $1,600, while the standard Part B monthly premium will be $164.90, and an annual deductible of $226.

Another medical expense you will need to budget for is dental expenses. Seniors often need crowns, dentures, tooth replacements, and other potentially costly treatments. These expenses mean you'll need some provision, whether a standalone dental coverage plan or Medicare Advantage.

- **Long-Term Care**

    While we all want to imagine ourselves living active, busy retirements, as we age, there is a higher probability that you will need to access long-term care. If you begin to struggle with health issues, which means you cannot live independently, you must cover the cost of long-term care.

    Unfortunately, this can add up to significant expenses. Depending on where you live, assisted living costs $40,000 to $100,000 per year. For many people, this amount will be above the recommended annual withdrawals from retirement funds, particularly as you will still need to cover some basic expenses. Many people are forced to sell their homes to cover assisted living costs.

    Fortunately, there are other options, including long-term care insurance. While generally, private health insurance will not cover assisted living, there are dedicated policies. Just bear in mind that these policies typically need to be purchased well before you will need them. So, it is well worth arranging a policy before you retire and budgeting the cost of the premiums into your retirement plans.

    Alternatively, you can save money toward your health care costs, including long-term care, with a Health Savings Account, also known as HSA. These accounts offer deductible contributions, tax-deferred growth, and tax-free withdrawals for qualified medical expenses. If you're already in your 50s, you can make catch-up contributions to maximize your HSA.

- **Life Insurance**

  If you want coverage for end-of-life expenses or to leave something for your family, you should budget life insurance into your plans. It is essential to remember that life insurance costs increase as you get older, so it is best to put coverage in place sooner rather than later. You will then have an accurate idea of your premiums.

- **Unsettled Debts**

  Ideally, you will clear your debts, but in some cases, it may not be possible or practical. So, if you have any outstanding debts before you retire, you must include them in your budget.

- **Any Other Expenses**

  Finally, you'll need to consider any other expenses you may incur. Now that you've thought about these expenses, it is time to write them down in this chart. This step will lay out your estimated post-retirement expenses, and we can move on to how much you'll need to save.

Expense	Estimated Cost
Housing	
Utilities	
Groceries and Food	
Clothing	
Entertainment	
Transportation	
Travel	
Health Care	
Life Insurance	
Unsettled Debts	
Long Time Care	
Other Expenses	
Total	

The 4% Rule

Once you have your estimated post-retirement expense total, you can apply the 4% rule. As we covered in the earlier steps, a good rule of thumb is to consider withdrawing 4% of your retirement fund each year, allowing a margin for inflation. If you have $1 million in your retirement fund, you'll have $40,000 per year to cover your monthly expenses.

Of course, you will need to calculate additional funds to cover savings and emergencies. But for now, you can calculate a base figure with this formula: the total of your expenses divided by 4 x 100.

This figure will show how much you need to cover your basic expenses, but in the next stage, we will need to look at other expenses you could consider.

Emergency Fund

Now that you figure out how much you'll need to cover your basic expenses, you can estimate what emergency fund you should plan for.

- **Why you Need an Emergency Fund:**

    As the name suggests, this fund is available for those unexpected expenses or financial emergencies. Many financial experts encourage having an emergency fund at all times, but it is essential when you're retired.

    The fund is there for expenses you haven't planned, like medical bills, vehicle repairs, or emergency home maintenance.

- **How Much Do You Need?**

    Ideally, you should have six months of your basic expenses as an emergency fund. So, use the figure you calculated above and multiply it by six. This information should be considered your base emergency fund figure. If you can afford to save more, you may feel more comfortable.

    To determine how much you need to save monthly to achieve your emergency fund, you'll need to calculate the cost across different periods.

For Example:

If your emergency fund needs to reach $10,000, you could follow these saving plans:

Period	Savings per Month
5 year	$166
3 year	$277
2 year	$416

You will need to consider the timeframe until retirement and how much you can afford. If you have ten years or more until you retire, you could spread the cost of saving for your retirement fund for a more extended period. If you are approaching retirement or have already retired, try for a shorter time frame.

Whatever timeframe that you use, you should save regularly. It is far easier to save $25 per week for several years rather than trying to save thousands of dollars in one go. Choose a manageable amount and commit to saving regularly, whether weekly, monthly, or per paycheck. This step will help saving to become a habit, and after a while, you may not even notice the amount coming out of your account.

t is also a good idea to automate the savings for your emergency fund. Set up a separate savings account, ideally one without easy access. This account will minimize the temptation to dip into your retirement emergency fund savings. You can then have an automated transfer from your primary checking account into the savings fund regularly.

Don't Forget About Tax

While seniors often qualify for tax advantages, you will still need to consider if you'll carry a tax burden in your retirement costs. After 72, you must make distributions from tax-deferred retirement accounts, or you could incur a 50% tax penalty.

You will need to calculate your tax liability if you have multiple retirement accounts or your retirement income exceeds a certain level.

Fortunately, some accurate retirement and withdrawal calculators can help you work out your tax liabilities, particularly if you plan on working after retirement. A good Example is this calculator from Robson Savage [1]. All you need to do is enter your fund amount, tax-free benefits, and a few other basic details, and it will give you an accurate assessment of the amount of tax payable when you retire.

Alternatively, you can create your own tax and retirement spreadsheet to work out your tax expenses. There are full instructions on creating your spreadsheet on the Spreadsheetpoint.com [2] website.

Saving for Expenses and Emergencies in Retirement

Now you have a figure for how much you will need to cover your expenses and any emergencies in retirement, you may feel overwhelmed. As discussed earlier, a realistic picture of your situation is essential, and knowing exactly what you need will help you.

Fortunately, some other factors can help you maximize your retirement fund if you're wondering how to save the needed amount. Many retired people will rely on Social Security benefits to supplement their retirement funding, but some strategies can help you maximize your benefits. These include:

- **Work for a Full 35 Years**

    Social Security eligibility can kick in after you've worked as little as ten years, and you can start receiving benefits from 62. However, with these parameters, you'll only be able to access the base level of benefits.

    Remember that you can postpone receiving benefits until you are 70, allowing you to add further years of working to your record. The average of your 35 highest-earning working years will be used as a base for your benefit amount. But if you have many years with zero earnings, it will reduce your benefits dramatically.

If you can wait until you reach the age of 70 rather than the minimum 62 to collect benefits, it will work out at an extra 8% per year! So, to maximize your benefits, you should work for a full 35 years.

- **Spousal Benefits**

    If you are married but have little earned income, it is worth investigating if you are entitled to spousal benefits. This option will provide up to 50% of your spouse's eligible amount. Even if you have divorced, both ex-spouses can claim spousal benefits, which are calculated based on the other's Social Security earnings. Just bear in mind that if you have since remarried, you will not qualify.

- **Survivor Benefits**

    Suppose your spouse or ex-spouse is deceased but was eligible for higher Social Security payments than you. In that case, you may be eligible to collect survivor benefits. It is possible to qualify for higher benefits if your spouse died before applying.

- **Dependent Benefits**

    This amount could be up to 50% of your benefits, and it doesn't decrease the amount you receive; it is added to the total amount the family receives. To qualify for dependent benefits, retirees must have dependents under the age of 19 in their household.

- **Watch Out for Mistakes**

    You receive a Social Security statement yearly, but don't simply put it in a drawer. You should not assume that the information is accurate, and you'll need to report any errors or mistakes to the Social Security Administration.

Since the Social Security Administration bases benefits on an average of your 35 highest-earning working years, a miscalculation in a year or two can impact your benefits in the long term.

- **Check for Earnings Limits**

    If you will continue to work after you start to receive Social Security payments, you will need to track your earnings. There are earnings limits; if you exceed them, you'll be penalized in your Social Security benefits. If you're below full retirement age, the 2023 limit is $21,240; for those above full retirement age, the limit increases to $56,520. These limits can change year on year, so check the limits each year once you start to receive benefits.

    You should also monitor your earnings to ensure you don't get hit with a tax bracket bump. If you're still working and receiving benefits, you could rise into the next tax bracket, negating your additional income.

Estate Planning

Finally, if you want to ensure that you have your plan for retirement in place, you should consider estate planning. Essentially, estate planning is putting your affairs to help your loved ones should you die or become incapacitated.

This step goes beyond simply creating a will, as it involves accounting for all your assets, including any unused retirement funds, and ensuring that they are smoothly transferred to who you wish, whether people or charities.

Although estate planning can be complex, there is a checklist to help you work through all aspects.

- **Create an Inventory:**

    You'll need to itemize all your belongings, including your home. If you have items that you want to leave to a specific person, add notes to your inventory along with pictures to avoid any confusion. Don't forget to list sentimental items, which may not have cash value but could hold a great deal of meaning for you and your loved ones.

- **Document Non-Physical Assets:**

    This is where you will need to start going through your finances and create a list of all your accounts. This step should include all bank and brokerage accounts, savings plans, and insurance policies. Include the account details and note where related physical documents are kept.

- **List Your Debts:**

    Have a separate list of debts or financial obligations, including mortgages, loans, and credit cards. Make a note of the account details and where any paperwork is kept.

- **List Memberships:**

    Make a list if you belong to organizations such as the VA, AARP, or a professional accreditation association. Some of these organizations offer members automatic life insurance benefits, which your beneficiaries may be able to collect.

- **Copy Your Lists:**

    Once you complete your lists, sign and date them and have at least three copies. One copy should be with your estate administrator. This person should be a responsible individual whom you can trust and who will administer your estate after you die. You should give one to your primary beneficiary and keep the last copy for yourself in a safe place.

- **Authorize "Transfer on Death":**

   Depending on where you live, your estate may need to go through probate before distributing your assets. However, you can designate many accounts with "transfer on death," which allows your heirs to receive the assets without the probate process.

- **Draft a Will:**

   Once you have lists of all your possessions and finances, you can document who you wish to receive them after you die. You can have an attorney draft a will in your stead or use online software to write your own will. The document should be signed and dated before two non-related witnesses, who will also sign it. After your will is notarized, keep this record in a safe place and let your loved ones know where they can find it.

- **Consult an Estate Attorney:**

   If your financial situation is complex or the process feels overwhelming, you should consult an estate attorney. They can also assist you with power of attorney, a living will, and healthcare proxy documentation.

Being prepared for the worst can help you plan for emergencies, and you can feel reassured that you have plans for your necessary expenses and unexpected costs. Now that you have a clear idea of how much you will need to save for your retirement expenses and emergencies, we can move on to the next budgeting step.

CHAPTER 5

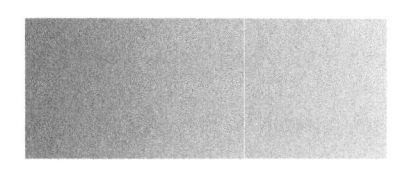

Budget Properly Through Every Step Before and After Retirement

"A budget is telling your money where to go instead of wondering where it went."

-Dave Ramsey

It's time to bring everything we've covered in the previous steps together. All the steps we've gone through will help you budget properly and manage your income. This step can be a rather daunting process; if you feel this way, you're not alone. In fact, research surveys show that 57% of adults dread the thought of budgeting, while 54% believe it is easier to follow strict diets rather than a monthly budget. Furthermore, one in four surveyed would rather tackle a 5K marathon on Thanksgiving than cut back on their spending.

The realities of budgeting can be frightening, but if you begin early, it can become a habit and routine. Regardless of your age, using a budget is vital to cover your expenses and cut unnecessary costs to enjoy your retirement. So, in this step, you'll learn the tools you need to effectively budget.

The Retirement Budget Basics

You may be wondering why you need to bother with a retirement budget, and the simple answer is that you need to have a full picture of your finances. If you are guessing that you should have enough money for your retirement, you'll never be able to fully relax to enjoy your golden years.

A retirement budget can create a blueprint for your spending and saving, so you can not only accumulate sufficient funds for your retirement but also spend with ease after you retire. If you've already budgeted for a vacation each year, you can relax and enjoy your break. Likewise, if dining out is included in your budget, you can enjoy socializing.

So, a retirement budget is not only a planning tool but can also provide you with peace of mind.

Creating Your Retirement Budget

At this stage, you'll need to bring your monthly expenses across from step four, your debt repayment and reduction plans from step three, and your preferred saving options from step two. This step will help you to understand how to budget for your goals.

To summarize, you will need:

- Your expected and surprise expenses you expect during retirement
- Your current expenses before your retirement
- Your income
- Any returns from working and current investments
- Your anticipated monthly savings

Once you have all of these figures, you can use a retirement budget calculator, which will help you to determine your income vs. expenses. This type of calculator will help you see how much you need to save for retirement.

There are many different calculators online, but most are simple to use. For Example, this calculator from Investopedia (9) requires that you enter your income and expenses, so it will present you with a pie chart showing what remaining funds you'll have each month.

Plan Your Distributions

When you reach a designated age, you will withdraw money or take distributions from your 401K, IRA, or other accounts. Planning how, when, and from which accounts you will take distributions is vital when creating your retirement budget.

You need to ensure that you don't withdraw too much, leaving your fund short, and avoid putting yourself at risk of tax liabilities. You need to balance your distributions with allowing your fund to continue growing.

It is important to note that traditional requirement accounts have required minimum distributions or RMDs. The IRS has requirements for when you can start taking money out of your retirement account, depending on when you were born. It is a good idea to speak to a professional advisor. Still, you can also get an understanding of the withdrawal requirements using the RMD worksheets available on the IRS website. Since any distributions will be taxed as regular income, the worksheets can help you understand any tax burden.

On the other hand, if you've been using a Roth account, you don't need to consider RMDs since there are no withdrawal requirements, as you've already paid income tax on those funds. Theoretically, you could allow your Roth account to grow and never touch it.

Budget Plans for Retirement: The Zero-Based Budget

A zero-based budget is designed to help you to spend all your money deliberately on paper. It rounds up the totals of your monthly income and deducts expenses until you are left with a zero balance. This plan can be helpful to ensure that every single dollar is used exactly as you wish.

Creating a zero-based budget is quite simple. First, you need to list your monthly income from your retirement accounts and identify your monthly or seasonal expenses. Then, deduct your expenses from your income to achieve a balanced budget with a total of zero.

You will need to list all of your expenses and decide how you will spend your money each month. With this type of budget, dividing your expenses into essentials, non-essentials, and seasonal can be helpful.

Essential expenses include groceries, utilities, home repair, and transportation. In short, essential expenses are anything that you need to live. Non-essentials, on the other hand, are things that are nice to have but you don't need. For Example, hobbies, gift-giving, subscription services, and even travel are non-essential.

Seasonal expenses can be essential or non-essential, but they are costs you don't need to cover each month. This type can include insurance premiums, property taxes, special occasion spending such as Christmas and birthdays, and auto registration.

You can use these categories as a starting point, allocating a dollar amount for each item on a month-by-month basis. You can then manage your spending until you reach a zero balance. Of course, as with any budget, you should track your spending to ensure that you remain within the allocated amount.

Examples:

- Lisa: Lisa has an after-tax annual income of $55,600, and her essential costs are $40,941. This calculation leaves her with $14,659 to cover non-essential costs, down to a zero balance.

- Bob & Mary: With their combined after-tax income of $122,000 and essential costs of $37,922, Bob and Mary have $84,000 to cover their non-essential expenses, investments, and other costs.

- Laurie: Laurie has an after-tax annual income of $30,600, and her essential costs add up to $19,242, which leaves her $11,383 for her non-essential costs from her after-tax income

- Helen: Helen has an after-tax annual income of $53,000, and her essentials are $26,091 per year, leaving her with $26,909 from her after-tax income to cover her non-essential costs and savings.

Budget Plans for Retirement: 50/30/20 Rule

Another budget plan which can be helpful for retirees is the 50/30/20 rule. This type is not as detailed as the zero balance budget, so you may feel it is a more manageable option.

This plan works on the principle of dividing up your income by 50%, 30% and 20%. 50% is allocated to those bills that you must pay. This allocation means that half of your after-tax income will be available to cover your obligations and basic needs. This fund should include groceries, insurance, utilities, and health care costs. If your essential expenses add up to more than 50% of your after-tax income, you will need to think about ways to cut costs.

The "30%" of your income is for "wants." This fund is for expenses that are not essential but things you want to enjoy your ideal retirement. This fund could include expenses such as eating out, buying a new car, travel, or anything else that is a little extra to make your life more enjoyable.

The final "20%" of your income is for savings and investments. This could include your emergency fund, unexpected expenses, or surprise costs. This last fund provides a buffer so you don't overspend and face financial difficulties.

If you want to save more and spend less, there is flexibility for the 20% and 30% allocations, but this is down to personal preference.

As with the other budget plans, you will still need to track your expenses to ensure that you stick to the 50/30/20 spending plan. You can track your expenses on a computer spreadsheet, budget planner, or even with a pen and paper if you're more old school. At the start of the month, take your income and divide it into 50%, 30%, and 20%. You can then add up the expenses in these three categories to stay on track. Just remember that you need to be working with your post-tax income. Your gross income may significantly differ from your net income, as taxes will reduce the amount you'll receive in your bank account.

Examples:

- Lisa: With this budgeting plan, Lisa's "needs" far exceed the 50%. In fact, her $40,941 need costs work out at approximately 80% of her after-tax income. This scenario means that she would need to reduce her necessary costs or increase her income to work within this budgeting model.

- Bob & Mary: Bob and Mary's needs add up to approximately 30% of their combined after-tax salary, which means they have great flexibility to use this budgeting system.

- Laurie: With "needs" adding up to approximately 65% of her current after-tax income, she would struggle to use this budgeting model. However, her new business should increase her income, allowing her to reduce her needs to 50% of her income.

- Helen: With Helen's needs adding up to slightly less than 50% of her after-tax income, she is ideally suited to this budgeting model.

Identify Your Expenses and Costs

With either budget plan, you will need to understand how to evaluate your expenses and costs. While many of us think that all of our expenses are essential, do you really need that gym subscription when you can exercise at home? Do you need to eat out when you can cook meals at home? Do you need that new item of clothing, accessories, or pair of shoes? Whether these expenses are essential or non-essential will depend on your personal perspective. Of course, some expenses are easy to categorize as "little extras," but others may be more of a challenge.

For Example, we all require clothing, but within this category, some items are necessities while others are wants. It's important to thoughtfully assess your expenses and categorize them as "essential" and "needs" or "non-essential" and "wants."

Once you have determined this, it will be easier for you to plan and manage your budget. You will then have a clear idea of where to allocate each of your costs to keep on track.

Tools to Help Your Retirement Budgeting and Tracking

While this topic can be daunting, there are some tools that can help you. These include:

- **Automated Transfers:**

    Automating can make the process of budgeting and saving simpler. By setting up monthly auto payments from your checking account to your savings and investment account and your service providers, you will ensure that you pay all of your essential expenses and put money into savings without giving it any thought. You will then have the money remaining in your account for your non-essentials and wants.

    Automated payments will also make it easier to review your budget, as you can go through your bank statements each month.

- **Mint:**

    Mint [1] is one of the most widely used personal finance apps that offers easier money management. The app is the creation of the same team that brought TurboTax to the market. Mint lets you connect your financial accounts to get a clear picture of your overall financial health.

The standard Mint app is free to use and has plenty of useful features. But you can upgrade to Mint Premium if you want access to advanced spending graphs and no ads during use. However, at either level, you can enjoy free credit monitoring so that you can track any changes.

Those considering retirement and retirement planning are likely to appreciate that Mint supports a variety of financial accounts, including bank accounts, credit cards, investment accounts, loans, and mortgages. You can also use Mint to monitor your spending and progress toward your financial goals. You can view recent transactions, upcoming bills, and your current balance. Interestingly, you can even set up alerts to avoid overspending or missing payments.

Best of all, Mint uses VeriSign and multi-factor authentication, so you can feel comfortable that Mint protects your account and personal data.

- **50/30/20 Budget Calculators:**

    If you think the 50/30/20 budget plan is interesting but lack confidence in your math, you should find a 50/30/20 budget calculator useful. A good Example is the calculator offered by NerdWallet [2]. All you need to do is enter your monthly after-tax income, and the calculator will automatically show you your 50%, 30%, and 20% figures.

    This setup means you only need to focus on your specific expenses and ensure they remain within the appropriate percentages.

- **Zero-Based Budget Calculators:**

    If you prefer working with a zero-based budget plan, there are online tools that can help you. While creating a budget plan using your preferred spreadsheet program or keeping a paper track of your budget is simple, there are some great online calculators.

    The zero-based calculator from DollarSprout [3] will walk you through creating your budget. To start, you will need to enter your monthly after-tax income. The calculator will then ask you to enter the appropriate figures for your expenses. Next, it will present you with a base budget to which you can add supplemental expenses such as groceries, gas, entertainment, and miscellaneous costs. At the end of the prompt, you'll see your budget breakdown, including how much you have remaining for savings and investments.

- **Retirement Outlook Estimator:**

    This tool is a simple online tool, which is also available as a free iOS app available on iPhone or Android. It can add some nice context to your retirement planning, tracking your finances and warning you if there are potential bad choices.

    To use the estimator, you need to enter your current age and retirement age. You must also provide other details, including your annual salary, current retirement savings, contribution rate, investment style, and monthly social security.

    After you click submit, you'll get a forecast with a choice of:

    - Sunny: Estimated to meet 95% or higher of your goal
    - Partly Sunny: Likely to meet 80% to 94% of your goal
    - Cloudy: Likely to meet 65% to 79% of your goal
    - Rainy: Likely to meet less than 65% of your goal

This layout is a fun way to get a good snapshot of whether you are on track with your retirement planning goals. Using the app, you'll also see suggestions on how your outlook could change if you altered your investment amounts during the year.

This layout makes it easier to play around with your numbers to see what impact it will have on your goals.

Tips for Effective Budgeting

If you're still feeling a little wary about implementing the budgeting techniques and tools we've covered in this step, there are a few tips that may be helpful for you.

- **Be Realistic:**

    Regardless of your chosen budgeting model, you need to be realistic about your income, expenses, and spending. There is no point in creating a zero-balance budget with spending categories if you will go into the red in a typical month or trying to squeeze your costs into a 50/30/20 budget if this is not realistic. As we touched on earlier, in our case study, Lisa could not use the 50/30/20 model unless she made radical changes to her finances.

- **Remember You Need to Live:**

    While saving for retirement and clearing your debts are important, you still need to live. Although it would be admirable to focus only on your essential expenses and cut all non-essential costs, this is not sustainable in the long term. If you attempt this, you will likely lose motivation, and there is a risk that your budget will spiral out of control. So, while cutting costs can be a feasible option, remember that you must have a good quality of life now.

- **Track Your Spending:**

    It can seem a little tedious, but it is very easy to lose track of what you are spending. So, keep track of your spending. Retain receipts for all your purchases and bills until you have written down on paper or in a spreadsheet what you have spent and in what categories. Don't rely on debit card charges on your bank statement, as you may have forgotten what each charge relates to when you view your statement.

- **Keep Your Budget On Hand:**

  It's all well and good to create a budget. But if you put it away in a drawer or a hidden folder on your computer and don't look at it again, you're not budgeting correctly. A good budget should be checked and reviewed regularly. In an ideal world, you should review your budget once a month or more to check that your spending and expenses are as planned.

- **Set Realistic Goals:**

  Motivation can be a major factor when making financial changes, so it is a good idea to set realistic goals when budgeting. In previous steps, you will have looked at how much you need for your retirement, but you won't be able to save this overnight. It is far better to make continuous progress rather than dramatic steps only to fall back.

Budgeting is crucial for successful retirement planning, so learning how to budget properly is vital.

Now that you've learned how to budget for your present and future finances, we can proceed to the next steps to assist you in enhancing your retirement finances and overall quality of life as you approach your golden years.

*I would like to ask for your help in sharing this
valuable information with others.
It will only take a few minutes.*

*By leaving feedback of this book on Amazon, you can help
new readers understand how they can plan for retirement even if
they don't have a substantial budget or are very close to
retirement age without the proper planning.*

*Please scan the code, scroll down to the review section,
In the Customer Review section, on the right side, there is this sign '>',
click it to show* WRITE A REVIEW *(in blue letters)
Then, enter your review.*

Thank you from the bottom of my heart.

CHAPTER 6

Retirement Plan Pitfalls To Avoid for Security and Wellness

"If we command our wealth, we shall be rich and free. If our wealth commands us, we are poor indeed."
— Edmund Burke

Now that you've fine-tuned your budget, it's essential to ensure you have a cushion in your budget to account for any missteps.

To check whether you are adequately prepared for retirement, it's important to regularly review your financial situation. This step allows you to confirm that you're staying on course with your retirement savings. If you find that you're falling a bit behind, you can make the necessary course corrections.

Mistake One: Not Being Properly Prepared for Retirement

You've already taken your first steps to avoid this mistake. But it is important to reiterate that you need to be properly prepared to enjoy a comfortable and stress-free retirement.

Retirement is like any journey, and just as you would if you were planning a vacation, you need to ensure that you pack properly and have enough in your budget to cover any missteps.

It is important to regularly review your financial situation to check that you are properly prepared for your retirement. This will allow you to check that you are on track with your retirement savings, and if you are getting a little behind, you can course correct.

Mistake Two: Underestimating Your Longevity

We've already included estimating your longevity in your retirement calculations. Still, it is always best to err on the side of caution. If you're 55 today, you will likely live to your mid-80s on average. However, there is also a small chance that you could live up to your late nineties or beyond.

Even if your relatives have a history of surviving until they are eighty, you may live beyond this lifespan. So, you need to budget accordingly. Life expectancy calculators are online, but these tend to use national averages as a base. A good Example is the calculator offered by the UK Office of National Statistics. [1] This calculator is super easy to use, as you just need to enter your current age and gender. You'll then see a graph showing your potential life expectancy, including the chances you'll survive to be 99 or 100.

These calculators don't typically include factors like family history or lifestyle. So, you will still need to use your own judgment. If you are in good health and planning to retire at 65, you should plan for up to 35 years of retirement.

It is also important to remember that if you plan to retire early, you must adjust your longevity calculations accordingly.

Mistake Three: Underestimating Cost of Living Increases

In recent years, we have all seen the impact of inflation on the cost of our everyday expenses. Inflation impacts food prices, gas prices, and practically every other essential and non-essential cost.

Unfortunately, inflation and the cost of living will not simply freeze as soon as you reach retirement age. So, you need to factor inflation into your expense estimates for your post-retirement costs.

Inflation and deflation rates result from the current fiscal policy. This information means that while in some years, inflation will be higher, in some, it will be lower. But overall, you can expect an average annual rate of 2%.

However, there are inflation rate formulas and calculators that can provide an estimate of the impact of inflation during your retirement years. A good Example is available from RocketMortgage [2], and it can give a fairly accurate illustration to help you make your retirement plans.

Mistake Four: Paying Excessive Tax

For many individuals, taxes play a significant role in income requirements and the overall retirement plan. You might believe that you've addressed all aspects adequately. However, it's important to acknowledge that we are just beginning to explore the intricacies of your retirement planning journey.

There are actually a number of retirement plan pitfalls you need to be aware of to avoid compromising your security and wellness. In fact, according to a MetLife survey, seniors lose almost $3 billion per year due to financial abuse. So, in this step, we will look at potential retirement scams, mistakes, and pitfalls you may encounter and how to avoid them.

Mistake Five: Falling For Retirement Scams

No one wants to fall victim to scammers, but it can be especially devastating for retirees. As mentioned earlier, retirees lose billions of dollars annually due to scams and financial abuse. Retirees can be particularly vulnerable to scams, as they are often looking to maximize their retirement savings and accounts.

There are three ways to avoid retirement scams: rejecting unsolicited investment contact, obtaining impartial advice before making an investment, and verifying that the company or individual you are dealing with is authorized and registered. However, some scams are a little more complex, so we'll now cover what you can do to avoid various scam tactics.

- **Charity Scams:**

    Whether there is a natural disaster or an event in your local community, you may want to help. Unfortunately, fraudsters understand this motivation to try to take advantage. The common tactic in this area is for criminals to call and ask for donations to nonprofit organizations looking to help.

    Oftentimes, scammers may request your credit card or bank account details under the guise of needing access to your funds. However, their true intention is to use this information to make unauthorized charges and siphoning off your money.

    To avoid this type of scam, you should not agree to give to charities when first approached, particularly over the phone. If you do want to support the charity, investigate which legitimate organizations are involved and find a contact number to call to make a donation yourself.

- **Estate Scams:**

    This type is one of the most despicable types of scams, which targets seniors as it takes advantage of the bereaved. Thieves may contact you after a loved one dies and you place an obituary notice. They will typically insist that your deceased loved one left a debt that must be cleared.

In some cases, the fraudster may attend the funeral services to learn more about you and your family before asking for the money to cover "unpaid debts."

Another type of estate scam is for someone posing as an employee of the funeral home calling to insist that there are additional charges that have not been paid.

In any of these scenarios, you should immediately refuse to send money. Ask for written documentation of the bill or debt, which you can verify.

- **Fake Government Scams:**

    Government imposters often call people posing as employees of the Social Security Administration or the IRS. They demand immediate payment of "unpaid taxes" or may ask for personal information for your Social Security or Medicare benefits to continue.

    There is often some sort of deadline or time pressure, often with the threat of a fine or a suspension of benefits. This scam often means seniors feel panicked about making an immediate payment or providing bank details.

    You can avoid running into problems with these scammers by remembering that the SSA or IRS will never initiate any contact via a phone call. If you do receive a call, it is likely a scammer. If there is a problem with your taxes or benefits, a government agency will contact you with an official letter so you can understand the situation and what you need to do to address the issue.

- **Medicare Scams:**

    This kind is similar to the above scam. But it is often someone posing as a Medicare representative offering some form of additional coverage, which can save you money. The scammer is likely to ask for personal details and financial information. In some cases, they may even have acquired certain basic details about you from your online profiles or other sources.

If you receive a Medicare-related text, call, or email, you should not respond. If you have any questions about your coverage, you should contact Medicare directly. They can also confirm the legitimacy of any deals offered to you in previous correspondence.

- **Grandparent Scams:**

    While you would think you could never fall for this type of scheme, grandparent scammers are extremely convincing. They often call, claiming there is some kind of emergency. They often sound panicked and claim there is a problem with which they need financial help. The scenario could be a car accident, a legal issue, or something they don't want anyone else to know about.

    These scammers are experts at harvesting information, trawling social media, obituaries, and other sources to get the details needed to make the call appear legitimate.

    You can avoid falling for this kind of scam by setting up code words that your grandchildren can use if there is a real emergency.

- **Internet Scams:**

    When you share details about yourself on social media platforms, you could become a target for online scammers. Internet scammers often find out personal details from your online profiles and use this information to craft scenarios that may encourage you to share more details or provide money.

    For Example, you may have shown support for the armed forces on your Facebook profile, or you could have posted about being a veteran. A scammer may then target you, pretending to be an army service person needing money to return to Afghanistan to visit their children.

If you receive a message asking you to share details about your personal identity, asking for payment, or requiring that you click on a link, you should delete it immediately.

- **Investing Scams:**

With this type of scam, a person may contact you claiming to be a real estate investor, wealth manager, or financial advisor, promising an exciting opportunity for big returns. "To participate in this investment, you will need to send funds now while there is still time," they will say.

If you send money, you will not see anything or receive any investment details. So, before you send any funds to a new investment, consult a professional, accredited investor and avoid making any fast decisions.

- **Reverse Mortgage Scams:**

If you own a home, someone may contact you, claiming to help you access some equity from your property via a reverse mortgage. While reverse mortgages are available, they are only offered by legitimate firms with the appropriate credentials. Scammers typically offer to appraise your home, which will incur a fee. Then, they provide you with an invalid valuation before asking you to sign up with shoddy loan documents.

If someone contacts you with a request to share details about your home or make payments to apply for a reverse home mortgage, don't respond. If you are interested in refinancing your home, you should discuss your options with a reputable lender or financial advisor.

- **Tips for Avoiding a Scam:**

    While we have covered some of the more common scams that target seniors and those on their retirement journey, there are some general tips to help you avoid any scams.

    Ask Questions and Check the Answers:

    Scammers rely on their targets, not bothering to investigate the situation before handing over any money. But, even if you question them, fraudsters are not incentivized to provide you with references, more information, or anything that will confirm the deal.

    So, take your time to perform your own independent research. Be sure that you understand the history of the company, the details of the investment, and the risks involved. Bear in mind that if an opportunity seems too good to be true, it probably is!

    Know Your Salesperson:

    Take some time to check out the person offering you an investment before you transfer any money, even if you already socially know the person. You should find out if the salesperson is licensed and if they have a good track record with regulators and other investors. Your state securities regulator (16) can allow you to check the disciplinary records of advisors and brokers in your area.

    Don't Assume Integrity:

    Good con artists can sound incredibly professional and have the gift of the gab. They can often make flimsy deals sound like a solid investment. When combined with a friendly demeanor and polite manners, it can be very easy to assume they have integrity.

    You should also be on the alert for salespeople who prey on your worries or fears. Behind the facade of friendliness and confidence, if the salesperson starts talking about how they understand the concern of costly medical expenses or the rising cost of living and how only their investment can help, you need to be on alert.

Don't Be Rushed:

One of the common tactics of scammers is to put you on the clock. "You need to act now; otherwise, you'll make a costly mistake!" Don't be rushed into making any rash decisions, particularly if the promoter is making recommendations on "confidential" information.

Be Wary of Any Unsolicited Offers:

When you receive an unsolicited phone call, text, or email about a company or investment but can't find any current financial information from independent sources, you should be very wary.

Fraudsters often reach out using these methods to try to tempt you into an investment or solicit funds for a scam. You should also be very wary if you are asked to transfer funds abroad. Offshore transfers are difficult to track and locate your money if something goes wrong.

Don't Be Afraid to Ask Questions or Complain:

If the person you're investing with is unwilling to answer questions or address your concerns, you should walk away. If you have suspicions about questionable practices or fraud, remember that you can file a complaint with state regulators, FINRA, or the SEC.

Mistake Six: Taking Out Loans Against Savings and Retirement Accounts

If you have an immediate financial need, taking out a loan against your savings or retirement account can be tempting, but this is usually a bad idea. While the loan application process is usually more straightforward with minimal paperwork, there is a great chance that the repayment will cost more than your original contributions, and you could lose money. A loan could also derail your investment projections.

If you have a financial emergency and a retirement plan loan is your only option, you should discuss the situation with a financial planner before proceeding. You will also need to evaluate the repayment options fully to check if there are better possibilities.

Mistake Seven: Overreacting to Market Volatility:

If you're relatively new to investing, the ups and downs of the stock market can be extremely daunting. However, market volatility is simply part and parcel of investing. Therefore, you should avoid the pitfall of overreacting to this volatility.

Understandably, you may feel distressed when the market starts to become volatile. But you need to be ready to react according to your retirement goals. You must identify when you need your investment funds, how much you need, and the importance of having that money. Remember that if your retirement date is still 10 years away, you have time to weather even big market swings.

You can also avoid overreacting by developing a proactive rather than reactive approach. Contribute to your retirement portfolio regularly, which means you invest when markets are low and are doing well.

If you're feeling uncertain, take time to avoid making rash decisions. Take a waiting period to reconsider your investment decisions, perform additional research, or speak with your advisor.

It is important to stay the course to avoid making bad financial decisions. If you are concerned, consider reducing your withdrawals. Selling investments during a volatile period can negatively impact your investment portfolio.

Anyone can make mistakes, but if you are aware of common pitfalls, you can tread more carefully and minimize any potential issues. While these retirement plan pitfalls can be scary, in our next step, we will start exploring how to build an income floor, which can provide you with more confidence. Creating a steady, small income during your retirement can help you ensure a happy retirement that gives you the money you need to facilitate your ideal plan for your golden years.

CHAPTER 7

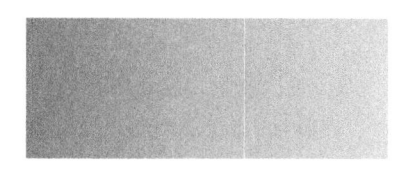

Create a Steady Income to Complement Your Retirement Years

"He who seeks rest finds boredom. He who seeks work finds rest."
— Dylan Thomas

While financial planning is essential and admirable, being able to generate an income after your retirement can provide you with some financial reassurance. These days, it is quite common for retirees to re-enter the workplace. In fact, a recent PayChex survey found that 1 in 6 retirees in the U.S. is considering whether to get a job. Whether from a need for more money, boredom, loneliness, or personal reasons, it is possible to complement your retirement years with a steady income.

Invest in Entrepreneurship:

Suppose you like the idea of maintaining your schedule during your golden years. In that case, consider starting a side hustle or developing an income stream by investing money into a new enterprise.

While any new enterprise requires effort, numerous ideas don't require years of experience or a specialized skill set. Some of the possible ideas include:

Expert Organizing:

If you enjoy organizing your home, you could turn this interest into your new enterprise. Professional organizers can help people to minimize and declutter their lives. Marie Kondo is the most well-known of these entrepreneurs, who helps clients downsize their belongings, only holding on to items that "spark joy."

If you're highly organized, you could help coach people to part with clutter to enjoy a minimalist lifestyle. Clients will pay you to help them with methods of organizing and maintaining their space. You can even use these projects for your portfolio, asking clients to allow you to take before and after pictures.

Food Trucks:

You could own and operate a food truck if you love cooking and food. There are food trucks in all sizes and shapes offering a variety of cuisines and snacks. You can take your favorite foods and share them with hungry customers.

While some costs are involved in starting a food truck, including purchasing the truck and modifying it to comply with local regulations and appropriate food certifications, the overheads are significantly less than opening a cafe or restaurant. You can also enjoy mobility, allowing you to serve food at events, festivals, and more.

Dropshipping:

For those considering a more traditional business but lacking the space to store goods, consider drop shipping. This service is a common strategy for e-commerce websites with a third party that fulfills their orders. This service is typically a wholesale retailer that operates a warehouse and shipping service, eliminating the need to hold inventory.

Dropshipping can be a great start-up if you lack physical space and want to keep your overhead costs low.

Podcasts:

Today, podcasts are incredibly popular, providing entertainment to those who want to listen to something on their commute while performing chores or simply relaxing. In fact, in the U.S. alone, there are over 100 million active listeners of various podcasts.

The great thing about creating a podcast as your new enterprise is that you can start one on practically any topic. Whether you're interested in pop culture, books, history, or business, there will likely be an audience.

To get started, you will need dedication and consistency, plus a basic understanding of editing audio and/or video if you want to support your podcast with a YouTube channel.

Once you have a decent following, you can find advertisers or partnerships to generate revenue. If you expand your brand, you can speak at events or become a panel moderator in your focus area.

Catering:

You could start a catering and event planning business if you enjoy cooking and hosting. Regardless of the time of year, birthdays, weddings, fundraisers, reunions, and other special events need delicious food.

To start, you will need to obtain the appropriate licenses and permits for your area. You can then set up your price sheet and sample menus. Once you have catered a few events, you'll likely find that word of mouth means your calendar will quickly fill up.

Airbnb:

Airbnb has been a boon for those who liked the idea of owning a cozy bed and breakfast but lacked the start-up capital. Airbnb allows you to rent out rooms to whole properties, so you can create warm and inviting accommodations for visitors to stay. This service is particularly appropriate if you live in a popular vacation destination or a place of cultural interest.

The platform is easy to use, and you can create your own listings with great photographs that will attract visitors. You can also specify when the accommodation is available and what amenities you can offer.

Tour Guide:

If you are interested in the history and sights in your local area, becoming a tour guide can be a great way to create an income stream and stay active in your golden years. As a local tour guide, you can share the sounds, sights, and flavors of places with visitors. You can even specialize in art-based, history-based, culinary-based, or other themed in-depth experiences.

To get started, you should take a reputable certification course to help market your skills. You can then list your tour guide services with numerous digital platforms to connect with customers.

Create Online Courses:

If you want to use your skill set and knowledge from your prior work experience but don't particularly want to work with clients, you could share your knowledge by creating and selling online courses.

There is a massive market for online learning, and there is a target audience for almost every type of course. You can set your own price and even get affiliates to help you to market and sell your course.

You can use a third-party platform to sell your course or build a website to promote your products.

Become a Specialized Consultant for Seniors:

With our aging population, there is a large market for specialized consultants who can help seniors redesign their homes to be safe and functional for independent living. You can also focus on life coaching or other aspects of independent living.

Depending on your area of specialization, you will need to look at appropriate certifications. There may also be some training involved. However, once you complete the mandatory requirements, you can market your skills and set your own hours for a flexible schedule that fits around your retirement lifestyle.

Senior Food Delivery Services:

While you may be an active senior, others struggle with food preparation and cooking. This service is where you could help build a lucrative enterprise. In addition to offering food delivery services to seniors in your area, you could help with grocery shopping, errands, and other everyday tasks.

Find a Part-Time Job:

While you may be keen to give up full-time work when you retire, a part-time job can be a good way to earn extra income and continue socializing with people. Of course, part-time hours can also be flexible, and depending on the role, you may be working a few hours a day or one or two days per week.

There are in-person, part-time job opportunities for both skilled and unskilled positions. Let's look at the roles with skill requirements first:

Tutor or Coach:

You can use your existing field of expertise to tutor or coach others. For Example, you could tutor in specific subjects if you're a teacher. This job can be a fulfilling way to use your teaching skills, as you'll work one-on-one with students.

Personal Trainer:

If fitness is a key part of your routine and habits, you could get a part-time job as a personal trainer. Many people assume that personal trainers need to be barely out of their teens. But older people may be more comfortable with a personal trainer closer to their own age.

Event Planner:

As an event planner, you'll work special events at venues or festivals. Even small events such as birthday parties can benefit from an event planner coordinating invitations, venue, catering, and guest services. This job is a varied role, as you could work for numerous events, including birthdays, weddings, anniversaries, graduations, and other special occasions.

Gardening Consultant:

While you may want to avoid tackling the hard labor of being a landscaper, a gardening consultant can still allow you to use your green thumb. As a consultant, you will help home and business owners create a landscape design according to their preferences, requirements, and land characteristics.

Personal Chef:

A personal chef works with individuals and families to craft meals to suit their preferences and dietary requirements. You could even create meals for dinner parties or home events. There are a number of companies that offer personal chef services, and you can work on a full or part-time basis.

Home Renovation Consultant:

Although there are project managers, a home renovation consultant works with homeowners to assist them with all aspects of renovation projects. This role can include explaining permit requirements to help design layouts and choose materials.

Bookkeeper:

These days, many businesses don't want the expense of keeping a full-time bookkeeper on staff. This job means they often outsource their bookkeeping needs to companies and individuals. As a bookkeeper, you could work in an office or from home, but you will still get to meet with clients, particularly during tax season.

Real Estate Agent:

As a real estate agent, you will be the primary point of contact for buyers and sellers. You will provide guidance on the process of buying and selling homes and making a commission on sales. You will also need to network and advertise to generate new business.

Art/Craft Teacher:

If you already hold qualifications for teaching arts or crafts, you could work part-time using your existing skills and experience. Many schools lack the funds for a full-time arts program and offer part-time teaching work. Alternatively, you may teach classes at community centers, retirement communities, and other venues.

Now, let's look at the part-time, in-person jobs for unskilled workers. These can be a good option if you don't have formal skills or don't want to continue working in the industry where you have experience or qualifications.

Retail Assistant:

As a retail assistant, you could be working at the front of the store as a greeter, assisting customers on the sales floor, ringing up transactions at the check-out, or even in a designated customer service area such as a gift-wrapping station. Another advantage of working in this role is that many retailers offer a staff discount, so you could save money on purchases from your favorite brand.

Pet Sitter or Dog Walker:

If you love animals, you could work part-time as a pet sitter or dog walker. Approximately 66% of households in the U.S. have pets. However, many people may not have the time or physical ability to take care of their furry friends 24/7. This is where you can help. This job can be varied and rewarding, from taking dogs for walks while their owners are at work to looking after pets while their owners are away from home. This job can also be a great way to remain active as you age.

Babysitter:

As a babysitter, you'll be responsible for the comfort and care of the children in your charge. You may be required when parents need to work, travel, or simply need a date night. You could work in the family's home or at a facility that offers sitting services, such as a church or community center.

Courier/Delivery Person:

Being a courier has become a popular side hustle for people of all ages, including retirees. There are numerous platforms where you can work freelance, delivering food, groceries, parcels, and other items. You can typically pick your own hours and work using your own vehicle.

House Cleaner:

The common duties may include sweeping and mopping hard floors, vacuuming carpets, dusting surfaces, removing garbage, and changing linens. You may be working in private homes, but there are similar roles in hotels and residential facilities.

Lawn Caretaker:

A beautiful lawn can make a property even more impressive, but keeping a lawn looking great can be challenging. A lawn caretaker specializes in this area, mowing grass, applying fertilizers, seeding lawns, and advising on proper maintenance practices. You may work for a lawn care company or offer services to private homes, businesses, and government buildings.

Product Demonstrator:

If you tend to visit grocery stores regularly, you are likely to have seen product demonstrators offering free samples or showing off merchandise in stores. As a demonstrator, you'll chat with customers, give out samples, and offer coupons according to the specific promotion.

Grocery Shopper:

These days, many people rely on grocery delivery. So, as a grocery shopper, you will pick products according to the customer's list. You may work with one grocery store exclusively, or there are freelance platforms where you can pick up customer grocery orders from different stores in your area.

Caregiver:

Seniors with mobility issues or the housebound often need assistance with everyday personal care. As a caregiver, you may assist with cooking, cleaning, and personal care duties. This job can be a fulfilling role as you are helping people in your community and assisting in improving their quality of life.

Uber/Lyft Driver:

If you enjoy driving, a flexible part-time job is as an Uber or Lyft driver. While these platforms have specific requirements, including passing a background check and having a suitable vehicle, you can pick and choose the driving jobs. You can also boost your hourly rate with tips if you provide a good service for your passengers.

Work Online:

If you have mobility issues or want to work from the comfort of your own home, you could work online. There are plenty of online opportunities for both skilled and unskilled roles. These include:

Online Tutor:

We've covered being a tutor above, but there are also opportunities outside the classroom. Numerous online platforms are continually looking for qualified tutors in a variety of subjects. Each platform has its requirements to qualify as a tutor, but some only require basic certification.

Social Media Manager:

Social media has become integral to marketing for businesses and online influencers. However, maintaining multiple social media accounts can be time-consuming, so many outsource this task to a social media manager. The tasks in this role include making posts, responding to comments, engaging with subscribers, and possibly coordinating sponsorship deals.

Virtual Assistant:

A virtual assistant is a freelancing role that provides support services for businesses and the self-employed. This job is a varied job with different responsibilities depending on the client. It could include responding to emails, scheduling appointments, writing content, etc.

Content Writer/Editor:

If you have a good grasp of the English language, you could work part-time as a content writer or editor. You can specialize in a specific area, using your experience from your previous career, or offer general services, writing blog posts, articles, sales pages, and emails.

Graphic Designer:

Graphics are an integral part of almost every aspect of business, from logos and website elements to marketing campaigns. If you have graphic design skills from your previous work or want to learn new skills, you could freelance as a graphic designer.

Translator/Interpreter:

If you speak multiple languages fluently, you could work part-time as a translator or interpreter. Many people need assistance reading documents or even understanding what they are being told in medical or doctor's appointments. You'll get to help people and keep your language skills sharp.

Financial Advisor:

If you have retained the appropriate certifications from your career or are willing to recertify, you could work part-time as an online financial advisor. You'll be helping your clients to find the best ways to achieve their investment, savings, and borrowing goals.

Remote Customer Service Representative:

Most companies have customer service departments, but more and more of these brands use off-site services. Essentially, when you send an email or use the chat function on a company's website, you will likely be dealing with a remote customer service rep. You must be friendly and have solid computer skills to work in this role.

Chat Support Agent:

This job is a little like being a remote customer service representative. But you'll be exclusively working via the website chat feature. Customers use company chat features on websites to ask product questions, query returns, or ask simple questions such as store opening hours. You'll need to be comfortable working on a computer and have good customer service skills.

E-Commerce Seller:

If you like the idea of being a retailer but don't want the overheads of a physical store, you could become an e-commerce seller. You will need a website to market your products and facilitate sales of your own or third-party items. As a seller, you will also need to deal with picking and packing, shipping items, and customer service issues.

Data Entry Clerk:

This job is a fairly basic role that does not typically require formal qualifications, skills, or experience. You'll simply need a good eye for detail and accurate typing skills as you enter the details you're given into the desired document.

Survey Taker:

If you enjoy sharing your opinions on products, services, and other topics, you may enjoy becoming a survey taker. This role can vary from quick surveys you complete on your smartphone or computer to participating in focus groups and forums. Numerous platforms offer cash, gift cards, and other rewards, which can be a fun way to supplement your retirement income.

Product Reviewer:

> Product reviews are a key feature for marketing items. The modern customer prefers to hear from someone who has used and tested a product rather than a wordy sales talk. As a product reviewer, you will receive and evaluate an item, providing a written review, which can be used on a company's website. The payment for reviews can vary from reimbursement for the item to cash or gift cards.

Online Juror:

> As an online juror, you can participate in the legal process from your own home. You'll participate in mock trials that law firms and attorneys set up to help their preparations for real court proceedings.

> In addition, you'll review the case information and make a decision as you could as a juror in a real court case. The feedback can help the legal team to test their cases and refine their strategies.

Virtual Receptionist:

> Virtual receptionists answer incoming calls and try to resolve basic customer issues, such as providing information and scheduling appointments. If the caller's issue is more complex, you will route the call to the appropriate department.

Telemarketer:

> Telemarketers make sales calls to potential customers. While this is often done from a call center, many platforms and companies now offer in-home work opportunities. You'll make calls from a list of leads following a script that the company will provide. You may earn a set hourly rate or work on a commission basis.

Content Moderator:

> Websites often invite users to post comments, but not all these comments are appropriate. Content moderators detect contributions

that may be insulting, irrelevant, harmful, obscene, or illegal. This job keeps the website content useful and informative.

Social Media Evaluator:

This role involves providing feedback on advertisements, search results, and news feeds for social media platforms like Instagram and Facebook. This job is a beginner-friendly job that does not need previous experience. You simply need to check the claims, realness, and quality of the content.

Microtasking:

If you prefer the idea of variety, micro-tasking may be more appealing. As the name suggests, micro-tasking involves completing very small tasks, which typically take less than two minutes. This job can include quick polls, checking images, and other basic tasks.

There are a number of platforms offering microtasks, such as Amazon Mechanical Turk. While these tasks are not high paying, they can add up to a nice little additional income since they require so little time.

Creating an extra income can be a great solution if you want some additional financial security. If you're unsure about what skills you can use to find a part-time job or start a new enterprise, tools like a skills matcher assessment [1] can help you. This tool is easy to use, as you need to answer some basic questions, and it can highlight possible opportunities for you.

Remember that retirement doesn't necessarily mean you need to stop working, particularly if you find an opportunity that complements your plans. Balancing work and life after you retire need not be challenging once we go through the remaining steps in this book, starting with learning more about self-care.

CHAPTER 8

Look After Yourself Physically and Mentally to Enjoy Retirement

"Take care of your body, it's the only place you have to live."
— Jim Rohn

Now that the financial side of a secure retirement is complete, you also need to consider your wellness, health, and ability to enjoy your golden years. Being active is recommended by psychologists, as spending too much time alone can contribute to both physical and mental health problems. So, in this step, we will explore how to plan and care for your retirement beyond savings and money.

The Facts of Wellness:

Before we go through the practical steps toward physical and mental well-being, you need an understanding of the concept of wellness. There are eight facets of wellness, and while we have already covered the financial and vocational aspects in the previous steps of this book, there are also physical, emotional, intellectual, environmental, and social aspects to consider. All of these dimensions need attention, as, over time, neglecting one or more facets will impact your health, well-being, and quality of life.

While achieving financial stability and savings control can contribute to the intellectual, financial, and environmental aspects of wellness, it's crucial not to overlook your physical, spiritual, and emotional well-being.

It's essential to bear in mind that without complete wellness, you won't be able to fully relish your retirement. In this step, you can ready yourself for spiritual and environmental wellness, with the final step concentrating on social wellness.

Physical Wellness:

Being active is important at any stage of life, but it is particularly important as you age. Physical activity can help you manage pain, maintain and even increase your balance and joint movement, control your weight, and address other issues, including diabetes, blood pressure, and cholesterol. Exercise can reduce your risk of stroke, heart disease, and some forms of cancer. Most importantly, physical activity can improve your mental health.

If you're planning on a relaxed retirement, you may feel daunted at the prospect of needing to be constantly on the move, but this is not necessary. According to the CDC, over 65 should aim for 150 minutes of moderate exercise weekly, which you could break down into 30 minutes per day, five days per week. This activity could be as simple as going for a brisk walk each day. Alternatively, you could perform 75 minutes of vigorous activity per week, such as running or hiking.

You should also aim for at least two days per week of activities that strengthen your muscles and improve your balance.

If you can meet these minimums, you can not only improve your longevity but also increase the time that you will remain fit enough to enjoy the activities you want to do throughout your retirement. This plan will help you to stay independent and enjoy a fulfilling life.

- **Staying Active:**

The great thing is that you can achieve these minimum recommendations with variety. Aerobic exercise, which can be vigorous or moderate, includes activities such as walking, jogging, dancing, and swimming. You can also use weights or bands to improve your strength, while pilates or yoga can help you with your flexibility. Remember that if you're new to exercising, you should check with your doctor before you begin and ease into the activities.

If you are unsure about how to get started, there are a few good suggestions:

    o **Get a Gym Membership:**

Gyms can be intimidating, but they are not solely the domain of those in their teens and twenties. A gym can be a great way to maintain your health and get in shape at any age. The benefit of a gym membership is that you can access a wide variety of fitness equipment. Depending on the particular gym, you may have access to exercise classes, a pool, a sauna, and other facilities.

With an array of options, you can find a fitness routine that works for you. This fitness plan could involve several smaller weekly workouts, taking some classes, or working with a personal trainer.

While the cost of gym memberships can vary greatly, there are often special deals for seniors. In fact, many gyms offer discounts if you are willing to limit the hours when you use the gym facilities, for Example, during the day, when many people are at work.

There are also often gym facilities and exercise classes at community centers, senior centers, and other venues that can provide a low-cost or free alternative.

- **Go On Wild Outdoor Adventures:**

If you enjoy outdoor activities now, there is no need to stop in retirement. Whether you enjoy kayaking, paddle boarding, or even ziplining, you can continue to enjoy wild outdoor adventures after retiring.

Just remember to consider the impact and your physical abilities. If you want to start a new outdoor hobby, check with your doctor before you start and seek advice on how to ease your way in.

There is no point in starting off with massive gusto only to suffer an injury or ache that will prevent you from continuing the activities. If you are new to outdoor activities, look for beginner- or senior-friendly classes to help you get started.

- **Plan Hikes:**

If you enjoy the outdoors but prefer not to be overly adventurous, you can incorporate physical activity into your routine through hikes. There are trails tailored to various fitness levels. Whether you opt for a gentle trail with minimal difficulty or challenge yourself with a strenuous mountain path that leaves your lungs working hard but rewards you with breathtaking views, there's an option for everyone.

- **Start Yoga:**

Yoga is well regarded for its ability to help relaxation and a sense of peace. However, yoga can also help you with your physical well-being, helping you to improve your flexibility and balance.

There are many types of yoga and ways to get into the activity. However, there are often senior-friendly, free, or discounted options at local libraries and community centers.

If you don't want to leave the house or are nervous about your skills, you could try an online course or a few YouTube videos. There are even chair yoga options for those who have mobility issues.

o **Do Some Balance Exercises:**

Balance can become more difficult as we age, but it is critical to health. If your balance becomes poor, you may not only feel less confident on your feet, but you'll be vulnerable to falls and their associated injuries.

Fortunately, there are simple balance exercises that can support mobility, strengthen your body, and reduce your risk of falling. These can often be done at home with a sturdy piece of furniture to support you as you stand on one foot or perform other balance movements.

o **Dancing:**

Whether you enjoy ballroom dancing or like disco, there is a music style and dance for all tastes and preferences. Dancing is not only enjoyable, but it is great cardio exercise. You can meet up with friends or make some new friends by taking dance classes or participating in senior dance events.

o **Wheelchair Exercises for Limited Mobility:**

If you have decreased mobility and are confined to a wheelchair, it doesn't mean you can't enjoy some physical activity. Although your movements may be limited, remaining physically active can improve your health and reduce pain.

There are exercise classes created especially for wheelchair users. If you're more adventurous, you could consider wheelchair sports like basketball or wheelchair racing. Even something as simple as stretching to touch your toes and extend your shoulders can be helpful.

The key to staying active is to find things you enjoy or activities you love and plan these into your retirement schedule. This plan will not only ensure that you remain physically active but enjoy your retirement fully.

Healthy Eating:

Another important aspect of your physical wellness is your diet. Older people are more likely to experience issues linked to nutrition. So, a balanced diet is even more crucial. Ideally, you should stick to healthier foods that will provide nutritional benefits. Aim to cut down on packed foods that typically contain high levels of salt, which can contribute to higher blood pressure. Your typical diet should contain lots of fruits and vegetables, adequate protein, and limited unhealthy fats.

If your working life has meant that you don't spend much time in the kitchen, now is the perfect opportunity to learn how to cook healthy recipes. In fact, this can be a rewarding hobby, as cooking can be fun, and you can impress your family and friends with what you learn.

If you're unsure about the optimal balance of nutrients, you could try meal planning, and there are a number of tools that can help you. These include:

- **My Fitness Pal:**

    This app is available on Android and iOS devices and contains the biggest food database of all fitness apps. There are more than six million different foods from a variety of cuisines and cultures. You can also scan barcodes from products and import recipes to find out the nutritional details.

You can use My Fitness Pal to monitor your calorie and macronutrient intake and check your progress against realistic health goals.

- **Yummly:**

   This tool is another app available on Google Play and the Apple Store. Yummly is an excellent option if you struggle with recipe inspiration for meals or easy and quick healthy snacks.

   There are more than two million recipes on Yummly, so essentially, you can browse the equivalent of multiple cookbooks. You can also personalize your Yummly profile to suit your dietary preferences or allergies.

   The app is really easy to use, as you can type in what you have in your fridge, and Yummly will provide you with recipes you can make with these ingredients.

- **Shopwell:**

   If you find grocery shopping tedious or struggle due to medical conditions, allergies, or other reasons, you should find Shopwell useful. This app helps to simplify nutritional labels so you can find the products that meet your specific requirements.

   The app also provides personalized scores for your nutritional food profile. This information can include health concerns, dietary goals, allergies, or even simply foods you don't like.

Emotional Wellness:

While the above points can address your physical well-being, it is also essential to consider your emotional wellness. Emotional and mental wellness is crucial to enjoying your golden years, but understanding it can be a little trickier. However, some expert-recommended activities have been proven to improve emotional wellness.

- **Stimulate Your Mind:**

  Just like your body, your brain also needs exercise. It is important to stimulate your brain, which can not only help your emotional wellness but also reduce any symptoms of cognitive decline.

  There are limitless ways to exercise your brain, from reading and doing puzzles to taking up a hobby or playing a musical instrument. You can take a class in something you're curious about or use your creativity to paint or work in your garden.

- **Get Good Quality Sleep:**

  Sleeping through the night when you are older can be more challenging. Disturbed sleep can impact your physical and mental well-being, whether it is a joint aching from being in the same position or needing to use the bathroom.

  Fortunately, there are some things that you can do to help you get good quality sleep, which include avoiding caffeine up to eight hours before bed, stopping drinking liquids two hours before bedtime, and making your bedroom as dark as you possibly can. You should also limit naps during the day to only 10 or 20 minutes. If your sleep is interrupted due to pain, ask your doctor about appropriate medication you can use before bed.

- **Practice Mindfulness:**

  Many individuals mistakenly assume that meditation and mindfulness are synonymous, but they are distinct practices. Meditation is typically done for a specific duration, while mindfulness can be incorporated into your day-to-day activities. Essentially, mindfulness involves being fully present in the moment, attentively observing your actions, emotions, thoughts, or words without passing judgment.

Research has shown that mindfulness can improve emotional well-being, physical health, and cognitive function.

Although the prospect may seem daunting, there are a few simple ways to get started. Firstly, set time aside from distractions, including other people and technology. You can also choose an activity that moves your body, where you can relax and switch off, such as walking outside. You may also want to try slowing down when you eat, taking smaller bites, and chewing more than usual.

Try to challenge yourself to be mindful of your surroundings and yourself so you can fully experience the present.

- **Meditate to Relax:**

Meditation goes hand in hand with mindfulness and can benefit your mind and body. Meditation can reduce stress, promote quality sleep, calm anxious feelings, and help with your emotional well-being.

You don't need to spend hours meditating to enjoy the benefits. Start off meditating for a few minutes per day, and gradually, you'll become better at it and enjoy it more.

- **Get Out More:**

Most of us feel more at peace when we're in nature. Getting out into woods, forests, and other natural settings can lift our spirits, soothe the soul, and revitalize us. In fact, in a 2008 study, a link was shown between living near or being in green spaces and improved mental health.

Since after you retire, you won't be tied to a full-time job, you can get out more to enjoy the great outdoors. Whether it is going for a walk and picnic or camping in summer, try to use your spare time and reconnect with nature.

- **Practice Self Care:**

    The term 'self-care' is a little nebulous, as it has a different meaning for everyone. The overall concept is to take time out to do something to improve your emotional and mental well-being. This timeout could vary according to your preferences and interests. But it should give you a feeling of well-being or peace.

    Even something as simple as sitting and reading or getting a pedicure can be good self-care. However, there are several ways to practice self-care. From enjoying a long, relaxing shower in the morning to taking a walk, self-care can take a few minutes or longer, giving you that sense of peace.

    If you're struggling to think about what self-care would mean to you, there are five basic concepts that you can use:

    - Get moving: Take a yoga class, go for a walk, join a fitness group
    - Make time for yourself: Meditate, read, journal, paint, or take up a hobby that interests
    - Head outside: Go for a scenic drive, visit a local park, or spend some time in nature.
    - Connect with others: Visit with friends and family, join a book club or community center, or take a class.
    - Give Back: Donate your time to a cause you feel passionate about or volunteer at a charity or local school.

    Self-care is a great tool to keep your stress levels low to help you to help you feel more relaxed and enjoy your golden years. Even simple activities like doing some gardening or brain training can provide self-care.

Think about what activities will make you feel relaxed. Think about the things that you daydreamed about before you retired. Are there activities that you wish you had the time for now? These can provide inspiration for your retirement self-care.

Jimmy Buffet once said that "wrinkles only go where smiles have been," and understanding what can make you feel a sense of peace and happiness will ensure you treasure those wrinkles throughout your golden years.

Getting your finances in order is essential for retirement planning. But your physical, mental, and emotional well-being are also crucial. The more you can care for yourself, the more you'll be able to enjoy your golden years. After all, there is no point in planning to have the funds to have a retirement spanning decades if you can't relax and enjoy yourself.

To truly make the most of your retirement, it's essential to remain active and physically fit while nurturing your emotional well-being to fully savor each moment. Once you've grasped how to take care of yourself physically and mentally to enjoy your retirement, you'll be prepared to delve into the realms of finding purpose and envisioning grand dreams to steer the best years of your life.

This journey will furnish you with a sense of fulfillment throughout your golden years without jeopardizing your savings balance or budget. We will delve into these concepts in the following step of this book.

CHAPTER 9

Give Yourself a Purpose and Dream Big Without Spending Money

"More smiling, less worrying. More compassion, less judgment. More blessed, less stressed. More love, less hate."

- Roy T. Bennett

Many people have grand dreams for their retirement. For Example, you may love the idea of traveling now that you are no longer tied to your work schedule and the restrictions of your annual leave. In fact, according to Visa research, approximately 25% of the 65 and older leave the country each year. However, finances can restrict your plans. In this step, we'll explore how to travel and find a purpose without taking a massive chunk out of your savings fund. This step will give you the tools to fully enjoy your retirement.

Finding Purpose in Retirement:

Before we delve into the specifics, it is important to recognize the importance of having a purpose after you retire. For many of us, our work is an integral part of our routines, lifestyle, and even identity. Just think about when you meet someone new at a social gathering. The chances are that one of the first questions asked is what do you do for a living.

Once you're retired, you will no longer have this identity, and this can lead to many people feeling lost. In a worst-case scenario, you may start to suffer from health issues and stress because you begin to feel disconnected from others. Even if you don't love your pre-retirement job, you are likely to get on with some of your co-workers and enjoy chatting with them on a daily basis. When you no longer need to go out to work every day, you can quickly start to feel lonely and adrift.

Many individuals may also experience disappointment because they haven't found their purpose, feeling that they should have already done so. There's a prevailing assumption that as a mature adult, you should have life all figured out. While you might have ideas and plans for your retirement, the absence of a clear purpose can lead to feelings of unfulfillment. If you find yourself in this situation, you're not alone. A research study published in Psychiatry discovered that in adults aged 21 to 100, people often found a sense of meaning in life after the age of 60. Therefore, if you haven't identified your post-retirement purpose yet, don't worry. The aim of this step is to inspire and assist you in uncovering your purpose.

Your purpose will be unique to you, providing you with a sense of satisfaction and fulfillment.

The Benefits of Finding a Purpose:

Having a purpose once you no longer have the 9 to 5 lifestyle can offer some great benefits that can enhance your retirement experience. Some of the specific benefits include:

- **Improved health**: Research [1] has shown that having a purpose has a very real impact on your physical well-being. In the study, the research team found that those with a higher score when rated for purpose had a 24% lower likelihood of being physically inactive, a 22% lower likelihood of developing an unhealthy BMI, and a 33% lower chance of experiencing sleep problems. It can also provide better outcomes for health issues, including stroke recovery and diabetes.

- **Improved physicality**: Research shows that a sense of purpose can impact your physical functions [2]. This activity includes factors such as walking ability, grip strength, and other issues that can enhance your quality of life and longevity.

- **Fewer feelings of loneliness**: Loneliness can be debilitating and may lead to mental health issues, including depression. However, if you have a purpose, you are less likely to feel lonely as you will have reasons for getting out to meet and speak to people and complete activities.

- **Protection against cognitive decline**: One of the biggest concerns among older adults is cognitive decline. For those with cognitive impairment, it isn't easy to enjoy an active lifestyle. However, purpose in life has been linked [3] to enhanced protection against cognitive decline.

- **Happiness and longevity**: Finally, there is a link [4] between purpose and feelings of happiness, which can impact your overall longevity and engagement in healthy behaviors.

However, while having a purpose is crucial, it can be counterproductive if it involves costly expenses that could derail your retirement plans. The golden rule is never to break your retirement budget, even for a purpose.

Finding Purpose in a Practical Way in Your Retirement:

Now that you recognize the significance of having a sense of purpose, let's explore practical ways for you to discover that purpose during your retirement.

- **Make a Connection with Your Authentic Self:**

    Spend some time getting to know yourself, what's important to you, and your overall values. As a mature adult, you are likely to already have a good understanding of yourself. But you need to connect with yourself on a deeper level. As mentioned above, many people view themselves in the context of their career, but this is a new phase in your life.

    Humans grow, change, and develop at every stage of life; retirement is no different. So, it is critical to consider yourself without the pressure of your career.

    Although this can be a daunting concept, you can start with some self-reflection questions, including:

    - What things make you who you are?
    - What things are most important to you?
    - Would things change if you were not a father, mother, neighbor, or employee?
    - What would you want your life to stand for?

To help you further, there is a list of core values you can study to see which apply to you or inspire you. These are:

Accomplishment	Accountability	Achievement
Adventure	Authority	Challenge
Collaboration	Community	Contribution
Cooperation	Creativity	Discipline
Encouragement	Equality	Excellence
Experience	Excitement	Family
Forgiveness	Freedom	Friendship

Generosity	Goodness	Grace
Gratitude	Health	Honesty
Humility	Humor	Independence
Influence	Integrity	Joy
Kindness	Leadership	Legacy
Love	Loyalty	Nature
Patience	Peace	Personal Growth
Pleasure	Potential	Power
Prestige	Purity	Respect
Safety	Security	Self Control
Selflessness	Service	Significance
Spirituality	Spontaneity	Tolerance
Travel	Truth	Variety
Vitality	Wealth	Wisdom

For Example, if one of your core values is family, you need to look at ways to improve connections with your loved ones. If you identify with generosity in retirement, you could explore the opportunities for volunteering.

> Core values can also provide a natural draw to people, places, and activities. This step means that if you do some introspection and connect with your authentic self, you will identify a road to finding genuine purpose.

- **Write Down Your Unique Talents and Gifts:**

    Everyone has talents or gifts which make them unique and special. To find purpose in retirement, it is important to recognize and share your unique gifts. For Example, if you have a gift of patience and teaching, your purpose could be to help others through writing books or developing training courses. If you have a gift for putting people at ease, you may find volunteering at a hospital or care facility fulfilling.

- **Explore Your Existing Relationships:**

    Examining your current, past, and potential relationships could hold the key to finding your purpose post-retirement. It is important that you surround yourself with people who can help you become a better version of yourself. So, it is a good idea to ask several questions:

    - Does this person energize or drain you?
    - Is this person encouraging or judgmental?
    - Do you enjoy spending time with this person or feel obligated?
    - Do you admire their lifestyle or want to emulate them?

    These people can become influential, encourage growth, support you through your challenges, or hold you accountable. But remember that other people can change just as you are looking to change.

    For Example, it is common for marriages to transition when retirement approaches. Differences can appear larger, frustrations can arise as you spend more time together, and it can feel like work. It is important to be honest and evaluate your relationship to see if there are new activities that could strengthen your bonds.

Ask Advice:

Meet up with someone who you admire and ask for their advice. This person can provide insight into your qualities and how this could lead you to your purpose.

Examine Your Passions:

Take a little time to write down your passions and interests. This step can help you discover what you want to do in a particular field or interest. Something you feel interested in now could become a major passion or purpose once you have more free time in retirement.

You should also try to identify what makes you feel happier. Happiness without any meaning will lead to a shallow life with no real purpose. So, highlight things, people, and activities that make you happy.

Share Your Talents:

Once you've identified your passions, interests, and skills, it is time to give back to the world. This action often leads to finding a sense of purpose and fulfillment. Some of the Examples of ways to share and give back include:

Join a Social Club:

Most communities have a social club where seniors can meet and spend time participating in a variety of activities. This step is not only an excellent way to socialize, but you can also share interests with like-minded people.

Volunteer Your Time:

As a retiree, you should have the time to focus on giving back. Volunteering for a charity or non-profit organization would provide meaningful activities and connect with your local community.

There are over 1.5 million non-profits in the U.S. alone, so you should easily be able to find a cause that interests you or that you feel passionate about. Volunteering can provide mental and physical benefits and should not involve spending money.

You will need to research which charities you would like to help in either a mental or physical way.

Some Examples include:

- **Meal Delivery:**

Meal delivery programs can provide a vital lifeline for those who cannot handle cooking for themselves. Usually, meal delivery is for seniors with physical issues that limit their mobility. However, you may also deliver meals to low-income households, those with disabilities, or as part of an outreach program.

- **Children's Hospital Programs:**

When a child is ill, it can be stressful for the entire family. So, hospital volunteers have a vital role to play. Whether you are helping out at a hospital clubhouse for siblings or some of the patients or being a guide to help visitors find their way around the buildings, this role can be fulfilling and rewarding.

- **Sort and Pack Food for Feeding America:**

Feeding America is one of the largest food banks in America, and it offers a variety of options for volunteers. You can garden, volunteer from home, assist at drive-through pantry locations, or sort and pack food parcels.

- **Volunteer Remotely for Non-Profit Clinics:**

The National Association of Free and Charitable Clinics has over 1,400 locations nationwide. They accept volunteers from a variety of backgrounds, from those with non-medical backgrounds to licensed healthcare professionals. However, you can also volunteer remotely if you prefer to work from home.

- **Mentor:**

There are a number of youth mentoring programs that can help children with educational tutoring, chaperoning, and other roles. You can still find a volunteer role even if you don't have an educational background or teaching degree.

- **Foster an Animal:**

When pet owners face health issues or other circumstances that prevent them from caring for their beloved furry friends, they often require a compassionate foster home. The ASPCA offers opportunities for you to step in and help save owners from the heart-wrenching decision of permanently rehoming their animals.

- **Host Local Museum Tours:**

If you love art and history, you could become a tour host at your local museum. This activity is ideal for those with an art background. But it can be suitable for those who feel passionate about art, history, and culture.

- **Religious Outreach:**

If you're religious and want to feel more involved or connected to your religion, you could volunteer at your local church, temple, synagogue, or mosque.

Travel Opportunities:

If one of your passions is to travel or you dream of seeing other parts of the world, when you retire, you can combine this with your desire to volunteer. Many volunteer programs can offer free travel and provide meaning for your life, which could open up your sense of self-fulfillment to a whole new level.

These include:

The Peace Corps:

You could serve as a Peace Corps Volunteer if you're a U.S. citizen. The Peace Corps helps countries meet their need for trained people, and your professional experience can make you an asset to your host country and fellow volunteers. You can use your skill set to help communities learn. You can also share your interest or passion, a hobby, a sport, or even inspire a new generation within the classroom.

The Peace Corps can provide the opportunity to learn about a new culture, see a new area of the world, and be embraced by a community that values your expertise and experience. The great thing is that you can even serve with your partner or spouse.

The Peace Corps allows you to select the country you want to serve in, when you would like to depart, and the type of work you want to do. Alternatively, you can choose where you are most needed, and the Peace Corps will aim to find the best position and country match.

Several Peace Corps programs could be of interest to you. These include:

- Peace Corps Volunteers: You'll serve for two years, but there is an additional three months of training. This program provides an opportunity for complete immersion into the community of your host country.

- Peace Corps Response: This program requires serving three months to one year in a specialized technical position. It is only open to those with relevant professional experience.

Considerations Before Volunteering:

Before making any decision to sign up for the Peace Corps, there are a few things that you'll need to consider. At any age, becoming a volunteer could impact various areas of your life. So, you need to evaluate the decision carefully. Included are:

Health:

The Peace Corps has important medical information disclosures for applicants, and all applicants must undergo comprehensive medical and dental assessments. These are necessary to ensure that medical needs can be supported with the available services in host countries.

A Peace Corps medical officer will be in-country to help you maintain and protect your health. This officer can also provide primary care when needed. If you experience a medical condition that requires levels of care unavailable in the assignment country, the Peace Corps can arrange medical evacuation to the U.S. or another country.

Social Security and Medicare Benefits:

The Social Security Administration is the only entity that can determine how or whether your benefits will be affected by serving as a volunteer. You will receive a readjustment allowance, and Medicare and Social Security payments may be deducted from this allowance.

If you choose to volunteer, you need to fully explore the implications of volunteering on your Social Security and

Medicare benefits. There may be unexpected tax implications that you should discuss with your tax advisor.

Technology:

There are many options to help you stay in touch with family members and friends while you're out of the country. However, if you want to maintain regular contact, you will need to check the levels of technology available in your assigned country. For Example, while 92% of Peace Corps volunteers have cell phone service, only 64% have internet access daily.

The Peace Corps can be a rewarding experience for volunteers, but it can also be challenging. You may need to develop language learning strategies, have less freedom of movement, and adapt to less structure. However, older volunteers typically find that their age can be an asset within host country communities, providing a unique experience that allows you to see the world and give back.

World Relief:

World Relief has approximately 20 offices across the United States, each offering unique volunteering opportunities. This program can vary from welcoming airport arrivals to helping resettle refugees, teaching ESL classes, and helping immigrants to apply for citizenship.

Americorps:

Americorps connects local, state, and national programs with citizens needing education, health, public safety, and security services. There are volunteer opportunities in these fields, and you can check the qualification requirements and options on the Americorps website.

IVHQ:

The IVHQ (International Volunteer Headquarters) has been operating since 2007 and provides safe, high-quality volunteer experiences abroad. This program allows you to choose the project, duration, and destination of volunteer experience. These programs are partnerships with local organizations helping communities in various projects, which can be a good alternative to the Peace Corps if you don't want to commit for a longer period.

Traveling, seeking adventure, and finding meaning in retirement can open doors to self-fulfillment and new opportunities. If you're among the many seniors who share the dream of traveling, it's possible to make it a reality without jeopardizing your budget or retirement savings. Discovering your purpose will also empower you to self-actualize and lay the groundwork for what comes next.

CHAPTER 10

Transform Your Legacy Into Inspiration for Others and Loved Ones

> *"Carve your name on hearts, not tombstones. A legacy is etched into the minds of others and the stories they share about you."*
> — *Shannon Alder*

The final facet of wellness that we haven't yet covered is your social well-being. In a research study focused on social isolation and loneliness in older adults, 43% of the respondents aged over 60 reported having feelings of isolation and suffering from loneliness. This issue not only has the potential to compromise your retirement plans, but it can also lead to mental and physical health issues.

To ensure your retirement goes as planned, you will need to seek companionship from your loved ones and new people, inspiring them to follow your retirement journey, entrepreneurial efforts, and financial stability.

So, in this final step, we'll explore how you can use the meaningful side of retirement to influence others and leave a legacy while enjoying a sense of social wellness.

The Importance of Social Wellness

Social wellness is a catch-all term for building healthy, supportive, and nurturing relationships and fostering genuine connections with the people around you.

Having an optimum level of social wellness will encourage you to build healthy relationships and develop a supportive social network, which can help to lift your mood and keep you moving, even as you get older. However, it can also have significant long-term health benefits. There is a link between an active social life and a decreased risk of developing dementia or Alzheimer's disease.

Ways to Remain Socially Active

Now that you can appreciate how much social wellness matters, let's discuss how to remain socially active with your loved ones and new people.

Bonding Activities with Your Spouse:

Retirement is a period of change within a marriage. After all, if you've spent several decades going out to work separately every day, being together 24/7 can be a massive change.

Many couples experience a need for adjustment, so undertaking some bonding activities with your spouse can be a great way to rekindle your relationship.

Whether this is scheduling a regular date night where you go out to dinner at your favorite restaurant or tackling a new hobby, spending quality time together is crucial. There are plenty of bonding activities you could try, according to your preferences and interests.

We've already covered the benefits of volunteering in the previous step, but this can also be a bonding experience with your spouse. If you both volunteer for the same organization, you can get the experience of working together and enjoy a sense of satisfaction from helping a good cause.

Other suggestions include traveling, taking dance lessons, joining a book club, or even playing cards.

Find Romance or Companionship:

If you're single, the prospect of loneliness can be even more daunting. However, you're not alone. The 2023 divorce rate for those aged 40 to 49 is 2.1%, while if you're over 50, the rate drops to 1%. This statistic means that at least one person in 1,000 couples will experience divorce later in life.

Fortunately, aging and divorce do not need to be the end of your romantic life. Rediscovering romance later in life can be a great way to fight the feelings of loneliness.

Although the prospect of finding a spark with someone as you're approaching retirement or after you retire can be daunting, you can start by participating in social activities or joining a group that interests you. This activity will improve your social life and increase the chances of meeting potential partners. There are also dating websites specializing in different age groups, including seniors.

Establish Multi-generational Bonds:

If you have been blessed with grandchildren, you will likely agree with the 72% of grandparents (1) who believe it is the most satisfying and important thing in life.

One of the great things about being a grandparent is that you get to enjoy the pleasures of engaging with your young relatives without all of the parental responsibility. You don't have to be the one who insists on them eating their broccoli. In fact, you can actually sneak them some sweet treats!

Intergenerational relationships can improve your quality of life and attitude, keeping you connected with trends and changes in the world. To create bonds with little ones, aim to spend one-on-one time with them. This bonding will not only show them that you love them as individuals but will also create a special bond that can be cherished forever.

If you don't have grandchildren of your own, try to bond with other youngsters in your extended family or your friend's children.

Teach an Inspiring Skill:

If you have a skill others admire, such as playing a musical instrument, try passing on this knowledge to grandchildren, children, or others. Music is not only good for improving your memory and providing well-rounded exercise for your brain, but it can be a great way to bond with others.

Making music with someone can help express thoughts, share feelings, and even create great memories.

Celebrate Your Family:

Celebrating your family can be a great way to create family memories and help bring your children and grandchildren closer to you and each other. After retirement, you'll have more time to reconnect with your family and kickstart new traditions.

There are a number of simple ideas to celebrate your family by starting or continuing traditions. These include:

- <u>Have a set date for a reunion</u>: Many extended families only tend to see each other at weddings and funerals, which can mean that you don't see each other for years at a time. So, set a date each year to have a family reunion. You could host at a different home each year or get everyone together to travel for a relaxing break.

- <u>Create a shared calendar</u>: Google and other online tools make it easy to create a shared calendar to include all family members' birthdays, anniversaries, and other special events. This setup will ensure that everyone is aware of when they are coming up.

- <u>Host family meals</u>: If you have family members who live nearby, host a meal each month where the entire family can gather.

Aim to find activities the whole family can enjoy, and you will make some superb memories.

Reconnect with Your Old Friends:

Reconnecting with your old friends, acquaintances, and former work colleagues is a great way to remain connected with your social circle. Whether you get together for a coffee or catch up over the phone, there are lots of ways to stay connected.

Set a dedicated time each month or week so you can catch up. Pick a place to meet up in person, chat over the phone, or even use technology such as Facebook or WhatsApp.

If you're no longer seeing your work friends on a daily basis, you may start to feel lonely, but you only have to look at people you've had relationships with in the past. Brainstorm a list of people and consider reconnecting with past coworkers, old college buddies, childhood friends, parents of children's old friends, and even neighbors, groups, and friends from previous neighborhoods.

Everyone has friends that they haven't spoken to or seen for a while. Whether they are across the country or live on the same street, make an effort to remain close to people.

Plan Random Surprises for Your Loved Ones

Most of us appreciate the truth of the old saying, "It is better to give than receive." Giving a gift makes us feel good and can improve our relationships. However, surprising a loved one with something you can do or enjoy together has far more meaning.

The great thing is that surprises don't need to break the bank, and you don't have to make grand gestures. Surprise a loved one with an impromptu dinner or picnic, write an encouraging note in a lunch bag, or spend time one-on-one. A random surprise can make someone you love feel on top of the world.

Celebrate Those Who Pass

Death is inevitable; you will lose people you care about and love. It can make it hard to know what to do with your feelings. Whether it is your grandparents, parents, siblings, or friends, these people are an important part of your life, and you will feel the loss for years.

While it may be tempting to stay occupied to distract yourself from dwelling on the loss, doing so may be a disservice to both yourself and your loved one's memory. Instead, try to embrace your emotions and navigate the grieving process by celebrating the lives of those who have passed. You can write a heartfelt letter expressing your appreciation for how much they meant to you or gather with others who are also mourning to share stories and laughter, commemorating the spirit of the person and honoring their memory.

Share Your Greatest Life Lessons

One of the benefits of getting older is that you will have learned how to overcome challenges and work through life's lessons. These learned lessons can help others when you share them.

Take a little time to evaluate what you have experienced and learned. Ask yourself:

What did you learn from any mistake?

- Did you do anything right?
- What could you have done differently?
- What things made a big difference to your life, even if they appeared small or insignificant?

Research [2] has shown that sharing life experiences can be beneficial for seniors and younger generations. Sharing can transfer wisdom, help to overcome pain, and could even lead to a rejection of stereotypes.

Sharing your golden lessons as you approach your golden years could help others and yourself.

Focus on Hobbies to Enjoy With Loved Ones

If there is a hobby that you can't wait to do after work or on weekends, this could be a focus for your social wellness, particularly when you can share your hobby with loved ones or friends.

Even seemingly solitary activities such as reading, cooking, or painting can become part of your social circle. You could join a book group, take or teach a cooking class, or take a painting class.

Write a list of past times and prioritize them in order of which you feel particularly passionate about. You could even include interests that you've previously not had a chance to explore.

Activities You Can Enjoy That Don't Cost Anything

Fortunately, there are plenty of activities that you can enjoy to create a sense of social wellness that doesn't break the bank. In fact, there are lots of activities that don't cost anything.

After you retire, you'll have free time to spend with family and friends, and you don't need to break the bank. Some ideas include:

- Play board games
- Play cards
- Join a bowling league
- Take up gardening
- Plan golf outings

Check out the available activities in your area. Community centers and senior facilities often offer free or very low-cost activities. Remember that when you coordinate plans with your family or friends, try to make them recurring. For Example, if you're interested in bowling, a league will ensure that rather than being a one-time activity, you'll socialize with a group regularly, which will provide structure for your retirement routine.

More Activities You Can Enjoy With Loved Ones

If you're still struggling with ideas for activities so you can enjoy with your loved ones, here are some more suggestions:

- Picnic: Whether you eat outdoors in your backyard or set up inside, a picnic can be a great activity for all ages, particularly youngsters. Small children can get a real kick out of spreading a blanket on the floor inside the home and setting up a picnic for you, the children, and any soft toy friends who want to join in.

- Classic Movies: Have a regular day or evening when you watch classic movies. It is a great way to introduce your loved ones to your favorite movies; they can reciprocate by sharing their favorite movies.

- Classic TV Shows: This extends from the previous idea, but why not revisit television shows from childhood with family members or friends? You can then talk about the shows and share some laughs.

- Painting or Coloring: You can have fun with adult coloring books or paint by numbers, sharing the hobby with friends and comparing your projects.

- Scrapbooking: Revisit old yearbooks, albums, and memorabilia to scrapbook. You can perform this activity alone and share the results with your family or undertake it as a group project.

- Create a Family Recipe Book: Why not create a family recipe book if family members ask for your recipes at family dinners or potlucks? You can document the family's favorite dishes with pictures, ingredient lists, and instructions. This book can be a great gift idea for family members, or you can create the book together.

Ways to Meet New People

If you're feeling a little lost and want to meet new people, there are several ways to help. These include:

- **Sign Up for Friendship Apps:**

    Many people find that making new friends becomes harder as they age, particularly as older adulthood has its own challenges. Once you're retired, you won't meet people in school, in the workplace, or at industry gatherings. However, many friendship apps can help you connect with people in your area or with shared interests.

    For Example, Meetup matches people according to their interests, while Pawdate app on iOS phone helps you and your dog to find new buddies. There are even apps to connect you with people in your neighborhood, such as Nextdoor. Most apps are free and can provide a solid way to enjoy social interaction.

- **Attend a Spiritual Retreat**

    If you're interested in making friends and getting involved in your community, consider visiting your local church, synagogue, or mosque. You can volunteer to assist with various activities, such as Sunday school, participating in finance committees, joining maintenance teams, or attending spiritual retreats. This can be an excellent way to connect with individuals who share your faith, fostering a sense of well-being and fulfillment.

- **Join a Walking Group**

    Walking groups can not only help you to remain physically active but also provide a way to connect with others and make friends. Walking groups can be highly social, allowing you to get to know people in your neighborhood and explore your local community.

    There are groups for all fitness levels, so even if you're not currently fit, you can find a slow-paced group that can help you to be more active.

- **Join a Book Club with a Focus on Self-improvement**

    Joining or starting a book club is an excellent way to make new friends, particularly if there is a focus on self-improvement. However, discussing books with those with similar interests over refreshments or morning tea can be the perfect way to socialize.

    If you need some help with topics of discussion for the books you cover, you may find suggested discussion questions in the back of the book.

- **Learn Something New**

    Taking a class in something you are interested in can allow you to learn a new skill and meet new people. Regardless of the class topics, you can discuss assignments with your classmates, socialize outside of school, and make new friends.

- **Meet Others Through Volunteer Work**

    We've discussed the benefits of volunteer work previously, but it can also be an excellent way to meet people. From volunteering at local charity shops or shelters to signing up with the Peace Corps, you'll get to meet people who share your passion, giving you a shared interest. It can be a superb way to develop a lasting friendship that extends out of the volunteer setting.

Remaining Socially Active and Leaving a Legacy

We've already highlighted the importance of remaining socially active and have provided plenty of ideas. Still, most people feel satisfied with the knowledge that they have left a legacy for those they want to inspire or influence.

There are many ways to approach this, including:

- **Find a Pen Pal**

  Having a pen pal you can write to and share your knowledge with can be a great connection and add value to their lives. You can support a pen pal through the challenges of their life, sharing your life experience to help them avoid pitfalls or problems you've encountered.

  Whether your pen pal is in your state, across the U.S., or even in another country, your correspondence can inspire them to live their best life.

  Some organizations can help connect you with a pen pal, such as Global Penfriends [3] and PenPal World [4].

- **Share Your Knowledge Through Mentoring**

  Mentoring, particularly when you mentor younger people, can be extremely fulfilling. You can use your experience and expertise to inspire young people. Having someone to believe in and look up to can be crucial, particularly if the youngster is vulnerable to crime, drug abuse, or other unsavory situations. A mentor can help youngsters create a plan to help them achieve their dreams, encouraging them into higher education and promoting a positive mental health outcome.

  Many organizations facilitate youth mentoring.

  For Example, Children Rising (26) has structured mentoring programs in the greater San Francisco area. These include tutoring in reading, math, and homework topics and high school youth mentoring. You can use your passions, hobbies, skill set, or expertise to volunteer in different capacities, guiding youngsters and creating a lasting legacy.

Steve Martin once said, "Be so good they can't ignore you;" this should inspire you to inspire others to leave a lasting legacy. Establishing your legacy can go hand in hand with your social wellness, helping you to avoid the isolation and loneliness that is far too common in older people.

By thinking about transforming your legacy into something that can inspire your loved ones and other people, you can enjoy a sense of fulfillment throughout your retirement years.

*I would like to ask for your help in sharing this
valuable information with others.
It will only take a few minutes.*

*By leaving feedback of this book on Amazon, you can help
new readers understand how they can plan for retirement even if
they don't have a substantial budget or are very close to
retirement age without the proper planning.*

*Please scan the code, scroll down to the review section,
In the Customer Review section, on the right side, there is this sign '>',
click it to show* WRITE A REVIEW *(in blue letters)
Then, enter your review.*

Thank you from the bottom of my heart.

CONCLUSION

The prospect of retirement can be daunting as we age. After all, many of us have dedicated most of our adult lives to work and careers, making the idea of no longer receiving a monthly paycheck understandably intimidating. However, the purpose of this book is to help you understand that ignoring this issue and hoping it will resolve itself is not a viable strategy. This book aims to provide you with the information you need to gain a clear perspective on your retirement and empower you to work toward your retirement goals with a ten-step plan.

Throughout this book, we've covered the importance of obtaining a clear understanding of your current financial situation and calculating the true cost of your specific retirement plans. While focusing on the future is essential, it's equally crucial to comprehend your current finances to make the necessary changes to free up funds that can be invested in your retirement accounts.

Fortunately, the process of planning your retirement can be broken down into ten manageable steps. These steps include evaluating your current finances, adjusting your savings, reducing your liabilities, and mapping out various aspects of your retirement, such as budgeting for unexpected expenses and finding a sense of purpose.

Even though this process is divided into ten distinct chapters, we've covered a great deal in this book. Be sure to revisit each step and work through the budgeting and planning exercises. Retirement planning can be complex, but the primary goal of this book is to boost your confidence in estimating costs, saving, and planning.

Retirement doesn't have to signify the end of an active life. So, don't skip revisiting the later chapters of this book. It's important to consider creating additional income through a side hustle, part-time job, or a new enterprise. This not only provides extra money to supplement your retirement income but also helps you stay socially engaged. Moreover, you need to pay attention to your physical and mental health, discover a sense of purpose, and learn how to pursue your dreams without compromising your retirement spending plans.

Retirement represents a significant transition for anyone. Whether you have a demanding career or a more home-based one, your attitude, lifestyle, and finances are likely to change when you retire. You'll need to consider not only the financial implications of no longer receiving a paycheck but also how to fill your days with activities that bring you satisfaction.

Whether you're nearing retirement age or just starting your career, it's never too early to begin planning. By following these ten steps, you can start feeling well-prepared and make proactive decisions to achieve your goals. Working through the chapters will also guide you in creating appropriate plans to ensure you remain on track with your savings and investments.

Learning how to maintain financial stability after retirement can be daunting and stressful, especially if you currently have a low to moderate income. It might be tempting to postpone thinking about it. But by using the practical tools provided in this book, you can plan the details and alleviate your stress. This way, you can save enough money for a fulfilling retirement, even in the face of financial emergencies.

Without proper planning, effecting any change becomes nearly impossible. However, by taking control of what lies ahead, you can begin to feel confident that you're continually working toward your dream retirement scenarios.

Utilizing the guidance provided in this book, you can empower and educate yourself for future choices and plans. By following the steps, you can craft a personalized outlook tailored to your needs, equipped with all the foundational tools necessary to plan for your best possible outcome.

Being well-informed is the most effective way to alleviate the stress of any situation, including retirement planning. Thankfully, you don't need to fret about expensive advisor fees or entirely sacrifice your current standard of living to save for retirement. After all, there's no reason to delay happiness, security, and peace until retirement. You can achieve balance and enjoy a quality lifestyle now while working toward financial security in your golden years through self-directed management and planning.

Financial concerns can affect people of any age, but retirees are particularly vulnerable to changes in the cost of living and concerns about outlasting their funds. Yet, managing your finances is just one aspect of a content and fulfilling retirement. Even if you have ample financial resources, you're unlikely to find fulfillment in retirement without considering your mental and physical health, giving back to others, and enriching the lives of younger generations who can benefit from your experience and wisdom. This type of legacy is invaluable and can bring profound meaning to your life.

I would greatly appreciate hearing from readers about how the information in this book has assisted them, so please feel free to leave a review or comment on the website you bought the book from. Your feedback may also aid others who are grappling with retirement and seeking guidance, much like you and I once did.

Please take satisfaction in the accomplishment of working through each of the ten steps in this book and constructing your retirement plans. By managing your finances and making informed decisions, you can look forward to a happy, secure, and peaceful retirement brimming with love and happiness.

REFERENCES

Notes: The references for each chapter start at #1, There will only be a few matched in the body of the chapter, the rest of the references are the information gathered to create the chapter.

Chapter 1:

1. Bank Rate. (n.d.). *Compound Interest Calculator - Savings Account interest calculator*. Bankrate. https://www.bankrate.com/banking/savings/compound-savings-calculator/

2. Ramsey Solutions. (n.d.). *Retirement calculator*. https://www.ramseysolutions.com/retirement/retirement-calculator

3. Gardner, L. (2023, April 10). *5 Steps to Check if your Retirement Plans are on Track?* https://www.linkedin.com/pulse/5-steps-check-your-retirement-plans-track-lee-gardner/#:~:text=Evaluate%20your%20current%20retirement%20savings%3A%20Review%20your%20current%20retirement%20savings%2C%20including%20your%20pension%20plans%2C%20individual%20savings%20accounts%20(ISAs)%2C%20and%20other%20investments.%20Check%20how%20much%20you%20have%20saved%20and%20estimate%20how%20much%20you%20will%20need%20to%20maintain%20your%20desired%20lifestyle%20in%20retirement

4. Today, K. F. U. (2018, February 5). 6 ways to measure if your retirement plan is on track. *USA TODAY*. https://www.usatoday.com/story/money/columnist/2018/02/04/6-ways-measure-if-your-retirement-plan-track/300912002/

5. Kagan, J. (2023, October 4). *5 Retirement planning steps to take*. Investopedia. https://www.investopedia.com/articles/retirement/11/5-steps-to-retirement-plan.asp#:~:text=Likewise%2C%20it%20is,high%20living%20standard

6. Gardner, L. (2023b, April 10). *5 Steps to Check if your Retirement Plans are on Track?* https://www.linkedin.com/pulse/5-steps-check-your-retirement-plans-track-lee-gardner/#:~:text=Review%20your%20pension,or%20property%20investments

7. *The National Council on Aging*. (n.d.). https://www.ncoa.org/article/14-steps-to-get-ready-for-retirement

8. *Paying off debt before retirement | Vanguard*. (n.d.). https://investor.vanguard.com/investor-resources-education/retirement/planning-paying-off-debt#:~:text=money%20for%20retirement%3F-

JD Williams | 141

,Your%20mortgage,to%20grow%2C%20which%20could%20benefit%20you%20more%20in%20th
e%20long%20run.,-Taking%20money%20out

8. *Paying off debt before retirement | Vanguard*. (n.d.-b). https://investor.vanguard.com/investor-resources-education/retirement/planning-paying-off-debt#:~:text=College%20loans,be%20tax%2Ddeductible

9. NerdWallet. (2023, November 2). *How to track monthly expenses in 6 steps*. NerdWallet. https://www.nerdwallet.com/article/finance/tracking-monthly-expenses#:~:text=Check%20your%20account,Categorize%20your%20expenses

10. Scutt, S. H. (2022, August 3). *What Does Longevity Awareness Do To Retirement Planning? - Pension Research Council*. Pension Research Council. https://pensionresearchcouncil.wharton.upenn.edu/blog/what-does-longevity-awareness-do-to-retirement-planning/#:~:text=Understanding%20how%20individuals,and%20limited%20attention

11. Kagan, J. (2021, June 24). *Longevity Risk: What it is, How it Works, Special Considerations*. Investopedia. https://www.investopedia.com/terms/l/longevityrisk.asp#:~:text=Understanding%20Longevity%20Risk,May%202021%2C%202021

12. RetireGuide, LLC. (2023, October 30). *Longevity Risk: How To Ensure You Don't Outlive Your Savings*. RetireGuide. https://www.retireguide.com/retirement-planning/risks/longevity/#:~:text=How%20Can%20Your,in%20the%20future

13. *The National Council on Aging*. (n.d.-b). https://www.ncoa.org/article/14-steps-to-get-ready-for-retirement

14. Today, K. F. U. (2018b, February 5). 6 ways to measure if your retirement plan is on track. *USA TODAY*. https://www.usatoday.com/story/money/columnist/2018/02/04/6-ways-measure-if-your-retirement-plan-track/300912002/

Chapter 2:

1. Patel, J. (2004, September 2). *Many Americans carry multiple retirement plans | PLANSPONSOR*. PLANSPONSOR. https://www.plansponsor.com/many-americans-carry-multiple-retirement-plans/#:~:text=According%20to%20the%20American%20Express%20Personal%20Economy%20Survey%2C%20slightly%20more%20than%20one%2Dthird%20of%20all%20individuals%20have%20three%20or%20more%20retirement%20accounts%2C%20while%20one%20out%20of%20every%20six%20people%20own%20five%20or%20more%20accounts%2C%20a%20news%20release%20said.

2. Kagan, J. (2023a, January 9). *What is retirement planning? steps, stages, and what to consider*. Investopedia. https://www.investopedia.com/terms/r/retirement-planning.asp#:~:text=SIMPLE%20Individual%20Retirement,goal%20retirement%20age

3. Bank Rate. (n.d.-a). *9 Best Retirement Plans In November 2023 | Bankrate*. Bankrate. https://www.bankrate.com/retirement/best-retirement-plans/#:~:text=means%20to%20you%3A-,Spousal%20IRA,Rollover%20IRA,-A%20rollover%20IRA

4. Kagan, J. (2023b, April 2). *Deferred annuity Definition, types, how they work*. Investopedia. https://www.investopedia.com/terms/d/deferredannuity.asp#:~:text=How%20Deferred%20Annuities,life%20as%20well

5. Best, R. (2023, October 18). *5 tips to increase your Social Security Check*. Investopedia. https://www.investopedia.com/articles/retirement/081616/5-tips-increase-your-social-security-check.asp#:~:text=Think%20of%20Social,Full%2035%20Years

6. Kagan, J. (2023b, January 9). *What is retirement planning? steps, stages, and what to consider*. Investopedia. https://www.investopedia.com/terms/r/retirement-planning.asp#:~:text=Employer%2DSponsored%20Plans,Retirement%20Account%20(IRA)

7. *Salary Reduction Simplified Employee Pension Plan (SARSEP) | Internal Revenue Service*. (n.d.). https://www.irs.gov/retirement-plans/plan-sponsor/salary-reduction-simplified-employee-pension-plan-sarsep#:~:text=%C2%A0%0AAdditional%20Resources-,Participate%20in%20a%20SARSEP%20Plan,age%2021%20and%20earn%20the%20minimum%20amount%20of%20compensation%20during%20the,-current%20year.%20Bob

8. *Employee Stock Ownership Plans (ESOPs) | Internal Revenue Service*. (n.d.). https://www.irs.gov/retirement-plans/employee-stock-ownership-plans-esops#:~:text=An%20employee%20stock,nonallocation%20year%20

9. Bank Rate. (n.d.-b). *9 Best Retirement Plans In November 2023 | Bankrate*. Bankrate. https://www.bankrate.com/retirement/best-retirement-plans/#best-investment-strateg

Chapter 3:

1. Loibl, C., Moulton, S., Haurin, D. R., & Edmunds, C. (2020). The role of consumer and mortgage debt for financial stress. *Aging & Mental Health*, 26(1), 116–129. https://doi.org/10.1080/13607863.2020.1843000

2. *Debt snowball calculator*. (n.d.-c). Vertex42.com. https://www.vertex42.com/Calculators/debt-reduction-calculator.html#:~:text=debt%20reduction%20strategies.-,Debt%20Reduction%20Calculator,for%20Excel%20and%20Google%20Sheets,-DOWNLOAD

3. Bareham, H. (2023, October 26). *How to calculate loan payments and costs*. Bankrate. https://www.bankrate.com/loans/personal-loans/how-to-calculate-loan-payments/#payments

4. Hartman, R., Marquardt, K., & Snider, S. (2023b, June 30). 9 reasons retirees carry debt. *US News & World Report*. https://money.usnews.com/money/retirement/articles/reasons-retirees-carry-debt#:~:text=Among%20retirees%2C%2071%25%20have%20debt,report%20from%20Clever%20Real%20Estate.

5. Birken, E. G. (2022, August 18). Retirement Planning: How To Get Out Of Debt Before Retirement. *Forbes Advisor*. https://www.forbes.com/advisor/retirement/retirement-planning-how-to-get-out-of-debt-before-retirement/#:~:text=Retiring%20with%20debt,retire%2C%E2%80%9D%20says%20Harrison

6. Loibl, C., Moulton, S., Haurin, D. R., & Edmunds, C. (2020). The role of consumer and mortgage debt for financial stress. *Aging & Mental Health*, *26*(1), 116–129. https://doi.org/10.1080/13607863.2020.1843000

7. https://www.meerkat.co.za/blog/financial-planning/retirement-savings-debt#:~:text=Before%20dipping%20into,more%20affordable%20premium

8. https://www.letsmakeaplan.org/financial-topics/topics-a-z/debt-management#:~:text=Making%20a%20plan%20for%20paying%20off%20debt%20starts%20by%20organizing%20your%20debt%20based%20on%20interest%20rate%2C%20terms%2C%20any%20tax%20benefits%20and%20other%20criteria.%20Debt%20management%20can%20help%20you%20figure%20out%20which%20debt%20to%20focus%20on%20first%20and%20how%20to%20lower%20what%20you%20pay%20in%20interest

9. https://www.moneymanagement.org/credit-counseling/what-is-debt-counseling#:~:text=able%20to%20help.-,Debt%20counseling,a%20day%2C%207%20days%20per%20week.%20Remember%2C%20it%E2%80%99s%20free%20to%20call.,-Review%20your%20finances

10. Kagan, J. (2023d, June 12). *What is debt consolidation and when is it a good idea?* Investopedia. https://www.investopedia.com/terms/d/debtconsolidation.asp#:~:text=some%20potential%20pitfalls.-,How%20Debt%20Consolidation%20Works,on%20debt%20consolidation%20to%20increase%20the%20likelihood%20that%20you%20will%20repay,-what%20you%20owe

11. Equifax. (2023). *How can I prioritize my debt payments?* https://www.equifax.com/personal/education/debt-management/articles/-/learn/how-to-prioritize-paying-off-debts/#:~:text=Short%2Dterm%20strategies,the%20snowball%20method

12. *7 steps to pay off debt and save for retirement*. (2023, March 23). Principal. https://www.principal.com/individuals/build-your-knowledge/7-steps-pay-debt-and-save-retirement#:~:text=Just%20as%20there,toward%20retirement%20savings

Chapter 4:

1. *Retirement And Withdrawal Tax Calculator 2023/4 | Robson Savage*. (n.d.). https://www.robsav.com/resource-centre/tax-calculators/retirement-and-withdrawal-tax-calculator/

2. Daniel, C. (2023b, March 2). 3 Useful Retirement Planning Spreadsheet Templates | SSP. *Spreadsheet Point*. https://spreadsheetpoint.com/retirement-planning-spreadsheet/#:~:text=less%20expensive%20neighborhood.-,Taxes,of%20your%20Social%20Security%20payout%20may%20also%20be%20subject%20to%20taxation.,-Things%20a%20Good

3. Today, R. P. U. (2022, March 25). A financial shock could wreck retirees' or pre-retirees' finances: Here's how to be ready. *USA TODAY*. https://www.usatoday.com/story/money/personalfinance/retirement/2022/03/25/retirement-prepare-sudden-financial-hardship/7157673001/

4. Borzykowski, B. (2022, September 21). The ultimate retirement planning guide for 2022. *CNBC*. https://www.cnbc.com/guide/retirement-planning/#how-much-do-you-need-to-save-for-retirement

5. RetireGuide, LLC. (2023c, October 20). *Average retirement spending in 2023 + Budgeting tips - RetireGuide*. RetireGuide. https://www.retireguide.com/retirement-planning/average-spending/

6. Retirement, V. (2023, August 24). *5 Biggest expenses for retirees & How to Minimize them — Vision Retirement*. Vision Retirement. https://www.visionretirement.com/articles/largestexpensesretirees#:~:text=happy%20retirement.-,Utilities,this%20AARP%20article%20on%2013%20ways%20to%20save%20on%20these%20expenses.,-In%20sum%3A%20how

7. Berger, R. (2023, February 19). What Is The 4% Rule For Retirement Withdrawals? *Forbes Advisor*. https://www.forbes.com/advisor/retirement/four-percent-rule-retirement/#:~:text=His%20paper%E2%80%94,in%20Bengen%E2%80%99s%20work

8. Cfp, K. D. (2023, March 23). Retirement vs. emergency savings: How to prioritize in a shaky economy. *CNBC*. https://www.cnbc.com/2023/03/23/retirement-savings-vs-emergency-fund-how-to-prioritize.html#:~:text=Valega%20suggests%20an%20emergency%20fund%20of%2012%20to%2018%20months%20of%20expenses%2C%20admitting%20she%E2%80%99s%20%E2%80%9Cmore%20conservative%20than%20most%2C%E2%80%9D%20but%20says%20the%20exact%20number%20depends%20on%20your%20career%20sector%20and%20personal%20preference.%20For%20example%2C%20she%20may%20encourage%20clients%20in%20tech%20to%20set%20aside%20more%20than%20health%2Dcare%20workers

9. Team, I. (2022, June 29). *How to build an emergency fund*. Investopedia. https://www.investopedia.com/personal-finance/how-to-build-emergency-fund/#:~:text=just%20five%20years.-,Where%20to%20Put%20the%20Money,The%20Bottom%20Line,-View%20your%20emergency

10. Securian Financial. (n.d.). *5 steps to build an emergency fund*. https://www.securian.com/insights-tools/articles/5-steps-to-building-an-emergency-fund.html#:~:text=2.%20Start%20with,monthly%20spending%20or

11. Probasco, J. (2022, October 14). *9 ways to boost your Social Security Benefits*. Investopedia. https://www.investopedia.com/articles/retirement/112116/10-social-security-secrets-could-boost-your-benefits.asp#:~:text=RETIREMENT%20PLANNING%20%20SOCIAL,%2C%E2%80%9D%20Page%201

12. Lake, R. (2023, October 23). *How to plan for medical expenses in retirement*. Investopedia. https://www.investopedia.com/retirement/how-plan-medical-expenses-retirement/#:~:text=What%20Medicare%20Covers%20

13. Shuman, T. (2023, November 9). *How much does assisted living cost?* SeniorLiving.org. https://www.seniorliving.org/assisted-living/costs/

14. Hopkins, J. (2022, June 28). *Long-Term care planning: It's about family*. Investopedia. https://www.investopedia.com/insurance/longterm-care-planning-its-about-family/#:~:text=The%20Complexities%20of,Impacts%20on%C2%A0Caregivers

15. Segal, T. (2023, June 10). *Estate Planning: 16 things to do Before You Die*. Investopedia. https://www.investopedia.com/articles/retirement/10/estate-planning-checklist.asp#:~:text=What%20Is%20Estate,transferring%20the%20money

Chapter 5:

1. Mint. (n.d.). *Budgeting: Online Budget Building Tool | Mint*. https://mint.intuit.com/how-mint-works/budgets

2. NerdWallet. (2023, October 18). *Monthly 50/30/20 Budget Calculator*. NerdWallet. https://www.nerdwallet.com/article/finance/nerdwallet-budget-calculator?trk=nw_gn_5.0

3. *Zero-Based Budget Calculator - DollarSprout*. (2021, May 24). DollarSprout. https://dollarsprout.com/zero-based-budget-calculator/

4. Today, N. G. U. (2022, July 1). 57% of young adults dread budgeting. Here are 4 easy ways to remove the stress. *The Motley Fool*. https://www.usatoday.com/story/money/personalfinance/budget-and-spending/2022/07/01/budgeting-for-young-adults/50435075/

5. Cepf, D. S. (2023, September 12). *How to make a retirement budget*. SmartAsset. https://smartasset.com/retirement/how-to-make-a-retirement-budget

6. Fontinelle, A. (2023, July 25). *Budgeting for the 4 phases of retirement*. Investopedia. https://www.investopedia.com/articles/personal-finance/110315/4-phases-retirement-and-how-budget-them.asp#:~:text=What%20Is%20a,The%20Bottom%20Line

7. Solutions, R. (2023, September 6). *How to create a retirement budget*. Ramsey Solutions. https://www.ramseysolutions.com/retirement/how-much-money-will-you-need-in-retirement#:~:text=2.%20Plan%20your,Required%20Minimum%20Distributions

8. Whiteside, E. (2023, October 10). *The 50/30/20 budget rule explained with examples*. Investopedia. https://www.investopedia.com/ask/answers/022916/what-502030-budget-rule.asp#:~:text=Utilities-,30%25%3A%20Wants,20%25%3A%20Savings,-Finally%2C%20try%20to

9. Folger, J. (2021, September 15). *4 top apps to track your retirement money*. Investopedia. https://www.investopedia.com/articles/personal-finance/041515/4-best-apps-track-your-retirement-money.asp#:~:text=Robo%2Dadvisor%20Personal,encrypts%20user%20data

Chapter 6:

1. *Life expectancy calculator - Office for National Statistics*. (2019b, June 6). https://www.ons.gov.uk/peoplepopulationandcommunity/healthandsocialcare/healthandlifeexpectancies/articles/lifeexpectancycalculator/2019-06-07

2. *Rocket money.* (n.d.-b). https://www.rocketmoney.com/learn/personal-finance/how-to-calculate-inflation-rate

3. North American Securities Administrators Association. (2020b, August 20). *Contact your regulator - NASAA.* NASAA. https://www.nasaa.org/contact-your-regulator/

4. Today, R. B. U. (2014, January 14). USA TODAY. *USATODAY.* https://www.usatoday.com/story/money/columnist/brooks/2014/01/14/retirement-scam-aarp/4393415/

5. https://www.charles-stanley.co.uk/insights/commentary/retirement-mistakes-to-avoid#:~:text=7.%20Falling%20victim,sort%20of%20retirement

6. *Rocket money.* (n.d.). https://www.rocketmoney.com/learn/personal-finance/how-to-calculate-inflation-rate

7. Scott, M. P. (2022, July 31). *Will you pay taxes during retirement?* Investopedia. https://www.investopedia.com/articles/retirement/12/will-you-pay-taxes-during-retirement.asp#:~:text=to%20your%20accountant.-,Standard%20Deductions%20for%20Retirees,are%20married%20filing%20jointly%2C%20married%20filing%20separately%2C%20or%20a%20qualified%20widow,-(er)

8. Hartman, R., & Brandon, E. (2022, June 8). 10 common scams that target seniors and how to avoid them. *US News & World Report.* https://money.usnews.com/money/retirement/aging/articles/common-scams-that-target-seniors-and-how-to-avoid-them#:~:text=to%20an%20attack.-,Charity%20Scams,Funeral%20Scams,-If%20you%20place

9. *Avoiding retirement fraud | Investor.gov.* (n.d.). https://www.investor.gov/additional-resources/retirement-toolkit/avoiding-retirement-fraud#:~:text=your%20retirement%20years.-,What%20can%20I%20do%20to%20avoid%20being%20scammed%3F,Ask%20questions%20and%20check%20out%20the%20answers.,-Fraudsters%20rely%20on

10. Team, I. (2022b, July 25). *Borrowing from your retirement plan.* Investopedia. https://www.investopedia.com/articles/retirement/03/070203.asp#:~:text=to%20check%20first.-,Repaying%20a%20Retirement%20Plan%20Loan,2,-If%20you%20are

11. Hopkins, J. (2016, January 16). 5 Tips To Survive Stock Market Volatility In Retirement. *Forbes.* https://www.forbes.com/sites/jamiehopkins/2016/01/16/5-market-volatility-planning-tips-for-retirees/?sh=258378476106

12. Michael Liersch, global head of goals-based advice/strategy at J.P. Morgan Private Bank. (2018, November 12). Take these steps to control your (over)reaction in the face of market volatility. *CNBC.* https://www.cnbc.com/2018/11/09/take-these-steps-to-control-your-overreaction-to-market-volatility.html#:~:text=Be%20proactive%2C%20not%20reactive.%20Make,systematically

Chapter 7:

1. https://www.careeronestop.org/Toolkit/Skills/skills-matcher.aspx

2. O'Brien, S. (2023, February 22). 1 in 6 retirees are mulling a return to work. What to consider before "unretiring." *CNBC*. https://www.cnbc.com/2023/02/22/1-in-6-retirees-are-considering-a-return-to-the-workforce.html#:~:text=Roughly%201%20in%206%20retired%20Americans%20say%20they%20are%20mulling%20over%20whether%20to%20get%20a%20job%2C%20according%20to%20a%20recent%20study%20from%20Paychex.%20On%20average%2C%20those%20%E2%80%9Cunretiring%E2%80%9D%20individuals%20have%20been%20out%20of%20the%20workforce%20for%20four%20years.

3. Vemparala, T. (2023, October 26). *26 Great business Ideas for entrepreneurs*. Business News Daily. https://www.businessnewsdaily.com/2747-great-business-ideas.html

4. Forstadt, A. (2021, October 14). *10 small business ideas for retirees*. https://www.uschamber.com/co/. https://www.uschamber.com/co/start/business-ideas/small-business-ideas-for-retirees#:~:text=Bed%2Dand%2Dbreakfast,and%20licensing%2C%20property

5. Siege Media, contributor to LegalZoom. (n.d.). *13 retirement business ideas*. Legalzoom. https://www.legalzoom.com/articles/13-retirement-business-ideas

6. https://www.indeed.com/career-advice/finding-a-job/best-jobs-for-seniors-over-60#:~:text=11.%20Tutor,an%20educational%20background

7. Cprw, T. G. (2023, November 3). 100+ Jobs for Seniors Citizens & Retirees in Demand in 2023. *Zety*. https://zety.com/blog/jobs-for-seniors#:~:text=Fitness%20Instructor.%20Know%20your%20way%20around%20a%20gym%3F%20Fitness%20instructors%20earn%20%2422/hr

8. https://www.wahojobs.com/article/social-media-evaluator

9. *Amazon Mechanical Turk*. (n.d.). https://www.mturk.com/#:~:text=MTurk

Chapter 8:

1. https://www.apa.org/news/apa/2020/self-care-older-adults#:~:text=Adults%2065%20and,their%20own%20mortality.%E2%80%9D

2. Stoewen, D. L. (2017, August 1). *Dimensions of wellness: Change your habits, change your life*. PubMed Central (PMC). https://www.ncbi.nlm.nih.gov/pmc/articles/PMC5508938/#:~:text=Wellness%20encompasses%208,live%20life%20fully

3. Events, L. (2023, April 27). *Looking after your physical health and fitness*. NSW Government. https://www.nsw.gov.au/community-services/seniors/what-to-do-when-youve-retired/looking-after-your-physical-health-and-fitness#:~:text=Related%20information-

,Importance%20of%20physical%20activity,Staying%20fit%20in%20retirement,-It%20does%20not

4. https://www.cdc.gov/physicalactivity/basics/older_adults/index.htm#:~:text=Adults%20aged%2065%20and%20older,of%20activities%20that%20strengthen%20muscles

5. *Ways to stay healthy in Retirement.* (n.d.). WebMD. https://www.webmd.com/healthy-aging/ss/slideshow-healthy-retirement

6. *Successful retirement: Staying healthy - Age watch.* (n.d.). https://www.agewatch.net/ageing-why-and-how/successful-retirement-staying-2/#:~:text=Aerobics%2C%20badminton%2C%20bowls,such%20%E2%80%98impact%E2%80%99%20activities

7. Meyer, C. (2023, October 27). *22 Activities to Improve your Health in Retirement.* Second Wind Movement. https://secondwindmovement.com/improve-health-in-retirement/#:~:text=And%20if%20you,try%20breaking%20up

8. https://www.arborcompany.com/blog/top-10-exercises-for-seniors-in-retirement#:~:text=You%E2%80%99re%20never%20too,Dancing

9. https://sensights.ai/top-free-nutrition-apps-for-seniors/#:~:text=This%20app%20has,helps%20in%20making

10. Atrio. (2022, June 20). *How Self-Care Can Improve Your Life in Retirement.* ATRIO Health Plans. https://www.atriohp.com/news-blog/2022/june/how-self-care-can-improve-your-life-in-retiremen/#:~:text=Ways%20to%20Practice,physical%20health%2C%20and

11. Experts, S. (2022, August 9). *5 tips on how to stay healthy after retirement.* https://www.linkedin.com/pulse/5-tips-how-stay-healthy-after-retirement-seniorexperts/#:~:text=Try%20to%20Relax,mind%20to%20wander

Chapter 9:

1. Kim, E. S., Shiba, K., Boehm, J. K., & Kubzansky, L. D. (2020). Sense of purpose in life and five health behaviors in older adults. *Preventive Medicine, 139*, 106172. https://doi.org/10.1016/j.ypmed.2020.106172

2. Kim, E. S., Kawachi, I., Song, M., & Kubzansky, L. D. (2017). Association between purpose in life and objective measures of physical function in older adults. *JAMA Psychiatry, 74*(10), 1039. https://doi.org/10.1001/jamapsychiatry.2017.2145

3. *Purpose in life may protect against harmful changes in the brain associated with Alzheimer's disease.* (2012, May 7). EurekAlert! https://www.eurekalert.org/news-releases/512180

4. Alimujiang, A., Wiensch, A., Boss, J., Fleischer, N. L., Mondul, A. M., McLean, K., Mukherjee, B., & Pearce, C. L. (2019). Association between life purpose and mortality among US adults older than 50 years. *JAMA Network Open, 2*(5), e194270. https://doi.org/10.1001/jamanetworkopen.2019.4270

5. Tigar, L. (2023, May 22). How to travel the world after you retire. *Real Simple.* https://www.realsimple.com/work-life/travel/travel-planning/traveling-in-retirement-tips#:~:text=Though%20trips%20for,geographically%20and%20financially.

6. Levy, O. (2023, September 22). Finding meaning and purpose after retirement. *Caring Places Management.* https://www.caringplaces.com/finding-meaning-and-purpose-after-retirement/#:~:text=Why%20Purpose%20Is,Stress%20Reduction

7. Meyer, C. (2023a, September 21). *5 Paths to Finding your Purpose & meaning in retirement.* Second Wind Movement. https://secondwindmovement.com/finding-purpose-retirement/#:~:text=The%20reality%20is%20that%20modern,why%20finding%20your%20purpose%20is

8. Levy, O. (2023b, September 22). Finding meaning and purpose after retirement. *Caring Places Management.* https://www.caringplaces.com/finding-meaning-and-purpose-after-retirement/#:~:text=QUESTIONS%3F%20CONTACT%20US-,Financial%20Considerations,Ideas%20to%20Support%20a%20Meaningful,-Life%20After%20Retirement

9. Coxwell, K. (2022, June 28). *Prepare for Life After Retirement: 6 Ways to Find Meaning and Purpose for this Stage of Life.* NewRetirement. https://www.newretirement.com/retirement/prepare-life-retirement-ways-find-meaning-purpose-stage-life/#:~:text=5.%20Identify%20What,Week%E2%80%99s%20168%20Hours%3F

10. Levy, O. (2023c, September 22). Finding meaning and purpose after retirement. *Caring Places Management.* https://www.caringplaces.com/finding-meaning-and-purpose-after-retirement/#:~:text=Volunteering%20with%20a,Attending%20Local%20Events

11. RetireGuide, LLC. (2023a, August 16). *Volunteering & Retirees: Types, organizations and benefits.* RetireGuide. https://www.retireguide.com/retirement-life-leisure/volunteering/#:~:text=The%20largest%20network,specific%20eligibility%20requirements

12. *Volunteering and retirement.* (n.d.). https://www.peacecorps.gov/volunteer/is-peace-corps-right-for-me/50plus/#:~:text=you%20are%20a%20U.S.%20citizen%20and%20at%20a%20point%20in%20life%20where%20you%20are%20considering%20leaving%20the%20workforce%2C%20thinking%20about%20retirement%2C%20or%20excited%20to%20make%20a%20change%E2%80%94and%20a%20difference%E2%80%94consider%20serving%20as%20a%20Peace%20Corps%20Volunteer.%20You%20can%20even%20serve%20with%20your%20spouse%20or%20partner

13. World Relief. (2022, August 29). *Volunteer opportunities | Make a difference | World Relief.* https://worldrelief.org/volunteer/?utm_source=google&utm_medium=cpc&utm_campaign=LM-WR-Search-GBL-Nonbrand-NAV-Get_Involved&utm_term=overseas%20volunteering&utm_term=overseas%20volunteering&utm_campaign=LM-WR-Search-GBL-Nonbrand-NAV-Get_Involved&utm_source=adwords&utm_medium=ppc&hsa_acc=3178627692&hsa_cam=12477599504&hsa_grp=118342019723&hsa_ad=624852474947&hsa_src=g&hsa_tgt=kwd-351504315767&hsa_kw=overseas%20volunteering&hsa_mt=b&hsa_net=adwords&hsa_ver=3&gad=1&gclid=CjwKCAjw_aemBhBLEiwAT98FMq9zXctexbjQcFOvD7xg_SN2LcqChPEG_FG=

SQYxNm3bCF9UYeGahxoCfBgQAvD_BwE#:~:text=US%20Opportunities,our%20volunteer%20network%3F

14. *Find a volunteer opportunity | AmeriCorps*. (n.d.). https://americorps.gov/join/find-volunteer-opportunity#/:~:text=Currently%20the%20following,note%20that%20AmeriCorps

15. Varoy, E. (2023, January 10). Peace Corps alternatives & programs like AmeriCorps. *International Volunteer HQ*. https://www.volunteerhq.org/blog/peace-corps-alternatives/#:~:text=your%20top%20choice.-,Where%20can%20you%20volunteer%20with%20IVHQ%3F,you%20can%20feel%20confident%20that%20IVHQ%20will%20be%20the%20best%20alternative.,-EXPLORE%20IVHQ%20DESTINATIONS

Chapter 10:

1. The Editors. (2019, July 16). *Surprising facts about grandparents - Hella Life*. Hella Life. https://www.hellalife.com/blog/family/surprising-facts-about-grandparents/

2. Gallagher, P., & Carey, K. B. (2012). Connecting with the Well-Elderly Through Reminiscence: Analysis of Lived Experience. *Educational Gerontology*, *38*(8), 576–582. https://doi.org/10.1080/03601277.2011.595312

3. *Global PenFriends - PenPal Club*. (n.d.). Global Penfriends. https://www.globalpenfriends.com/

4. https://www.penpalworld.com/
   Welcome to PenPal World. (n.d.-b). https://www.penpalworld.com/

5. *Volunteer - Children rising*. (2023, August 4). Children Rising. https://www.children-rising.org/volunteer/#:~:text=We%20invite%20YOU,East%20Bay%20community

6. Abrams, Z. (2020, March 27). Psychologists emphasize more self-care for older adults. *https://www.apa.org*. https://www.apa.org/news/apa/2020/self-care-older-adults#:~:text=Molitor%20says%20many,Academies%20Press%2C%202020).

7. Meyer, C. (2023b, September 21). *22 Ways to Improve Your Social Life After Retirement*. Second Wind Movement. https://secondwindmovement.com/social-life-after-retirement/#:~:text=The%20best%20way,along%20the%20way

8. StoryPoint Group & StoryPoint Group, Senior Care Experts. (2023, May 31). *Retirement Activities: 30+ ideas for everyone's lifestyle*. StoryPoint Senior Living. https://www.storypoint.com/resources/health-wellness/best-retirement-activities/#:~:text=Prioritize%20Your%20Hobbies,chance%20to%20explore

9. *40 activity ideas to spend time with family and seniors*. (n.d.). https://seniorsbluebook.com/articles/40-activity-ideas-to-spend-time-with-family-and-seniors#:~:text=Have%20your%20senior,book%20for%20the

10. Anglicare. (2023, June 1). *7 simple ways to stay active and social in retirement| Anglicare*. https://www.anglicare.org.au/media-centre/blog/7-simple-ways-to-stay-active-and-social-in-retirement/#:~:text=Joining%20a%20walking,have%20to%20offer

11. *Mentoring for Kids: 5 Ways to Be an Effective Mentor*. (n.d.). https://www.bgca.org/news-stories/2021/January/Mentoring-for-Kids-5-Ways-to-Be-an-Effective-Mentor#:~:text=Give%20More%20Kids,help%20guide%20them

12. *Volunteer - Children rising*. (2023, August 4). Children Rising. https://www.children-rising.org/volunteer/#:~:text=We%20invite%20YOU,East%20Bay%20community

13. *Family and Social Influences – Cheryl Pence, PhD*. (n.d.). https://cherylpence.com/family-and-social-influences#:~:text=Chart%20Out%20Your%20Influences,life%20to%20discourage%20you

Printed in Great Britain
by Amazon